TEACHING IMPROV IN YOUR JAZZ ENSEMBLE

A Complete Guide for Music Educators

Zachary B. Poulter

Published in partnership with MENC:
The National Association for Music Education
Frances S. Ponick, Executive Editor

Rowman & Littlefield Education
Lanham • New York • Toronto • Plymouth, UK

Published in partnership with
MENC: The National Association for Music Education

Published in the United States of America
by Rowman & Littlefield Education
A Division of Rowman & Littlefield Publishers, Inc.
A wholly owned subsidary of The Rowman & Littlefield Publishing Group, Inc.
4501 Forbes Boulevard, Suite 200, Lanham, Maryland 20706
www.rowmaneducation.com

Estover Road
Plymouth PL6 7PY
United Kingdom

British Library Cataloguing in Publication Information Available

Library of Congress Cataloging-in-Publication Data

Poulter, Zachary B.
  Teaching improv in your jazz ensemble : a complete guide for music educators / Zachary B. Poulter.
     p. cm.
  "Published in partnership with MENC, the National Association for Music Education."
  Includes bibliographical references (p.   )
  ISBN-13: 978-1-57886-817-9 (cloth : alk. paper)
  ISBN-10: 1-57886-817-3 (cloth : alk. paper)
  ISBN-13: 978-1-57886-818-6 (pbk. : alk. paper)
  ISBN-10: 1-57886-818-1 (pbk. : alk. paper)
  1. Improvisation (Music) 2. Jazz—Instruction and study. I. Title.
MT68.P68 2008
785.065'136—dc22   2008003249

⊚™ The paper used in this publication meets the minimum requirements of
the American National Standard for Information Sciences—Permanence of
Paper for Printed Library Materials, ANSI/NISO Z39.48-1992.
Manufactured in the United States of America.

CONTENTS

FOREWORD

Once upon a time, people thought improvisation skills came from nature, not nurture. A kid was born that way—right? Wrong. And as a jazz educator, you probably already know that, and this book can show you how to successfully teach students the art of improvisation through an ensemble experience. Even if you still think kids can't learn to improvise, this book will help you and your students enjoy creating and exploring jazz in the classroom a whole lot more.

A complete picture of the goals, techniques, and desired results of teaching improvisation in jazz ensemble, this book can help you plan instruction, purchase jazz ensemble charts, and assess improvisation. An extensive list of resources will help you find useful materials, and the section on rehearsal techniques will be of special interest. You'll find improvisation techniques and suggestions for standards and assessments that connect the entire process of learning how to improvise with methods used by professional improvisers and that follow research-based recommendations.

The book discusses why and how improvisation can be integrated into the jazz ensemble rehearsal with specific rehearsal techniques derived from professional jazz combos. With the suggested standards and assessments, you can make improvisation a true part of the learning environment in your classroom through this sound and enjoyable curriculum and monitor and report student progress as well.

The sections on the nature and value of improvisation and the evolution of jazz in education will be of special interest to those involved in teacher preparation.

The lessons follow a logical sequence of instruction for students learning how to improvise. You'll find the scales, chords, and harmonic progressions that are most essential for jazz improvisers and suggestions for a sequence of instruction that emphasizes aural considerations and incremental technical difficulty.

What I liked most about the book is the emphasis on correlating the teaching of improvisation with the rehearsal of specific jazz ensemble charts.

As you know, jazz music publishers grade and advertise their charts primarily according to the difficulty of the written material, but as an educator you also need to consider the improvisational difficulty of a chart. Because the charts are the primary curriculum of most jazz ensembles, the unpredictability and inconsistency of their improvisational content seriously undermine effective improvisation instruction.

Although jazz improvisation instruction typically begins in an ensemble setting, no existing resource identifies or classifies the improvisational content of the jazz ensemble charts. Now you can determine the improvisational content of the charts prior to purchasing them. A rating system of improvisational difficulty and a corresponding sequence of instruction, correlated with a detailed catalog of jazz ensemble charts (jazz standards) currently in print, gives you the power to plan a logical sequence of improvisation instruction and reinforce it with performance charts that contain the same improvisational demands. Because the catalog lists separate ratings for the difficulty of the notated and improvisational sections of each chart, you can find charts with appropriate technical challenges in both notated and improvisation elements. A complete lead sheet for each chart shows the exact chord changes of the improvised sections.

You will enjoy creating and experiencing jazz at a higher level through this unique program, and your students will find that jazz improvisation is both exciting and rewarding.

—Willie Hill, Ph.D.
Director, University of Massachusetts Amherst Fine Arts Center;
Professor of Music Education, Former President, MENC,
Former President, International Association of Jazz Educators

ACKNOWLEDGMENTS

Many teachers have mentored me in the art of improvisation and also in the education profession. In particular, I am truly grateful for the patient insights and encouragement of Doug Wareing, Larry Smith, Wilson Brown, Gordon Jessop, Donald Peterson, and Ray Smith.

My research for this particular book benefited from the considerable insight and perspective of Shelton Berg (University of Miami), Scott Wilson (Snow College), and Ray Smith (Brigham Young University). Thanks also to faculty members of the University of Utah: Mark Ely, April Greenan, Joelle Lien, and Henry Wolking, each of whom both encouraged and challenged me to my benefit.

This book would not have been possible without the charts. My deepest admiration and thanks to the composers and arrangers who penned the music discussed in the book. My sincere thanks also goes to Mary Green and her staff at J. W. Pepper Music in Murray, Utah, for their invaluable assistance and professionalism. They graciously provided all of the charts I reviewed.

Part I

BACKGROUND INFORMATION

①

THE VALUE AND NATURE
OF IMPROVISATION

Jazz, America's great art form, owes much of its distinctness and vitality to improvisation. Similarly, jazz education reaches its full potential only when improvisation is a central emphasis of instruction.

But improvisation can be a slippery subject to teach. Especially in the jazz ensemble, the divergent ideals of free individual expression and full-ensemble unity must somehow be reconciled. Partly due to imperfect curricular resources and the instructional inefficiencies that follow, a focus on improvisation threatens to detract from the other pressing realities of an educational jazz program, like preparing for frequent concerts and assessing and documenting student achievement.

However, when approached properly, the teaching of improvisation in jazz ensembles has a synergistic effect, energizing student learning while providing the large ensemble with its most thrilling performance moments. The vital resources that can either facilitate or destroy this type of experience are the jazz ensemble charts (arrangements and compositions).

By carefully choosing jazz ensemble charts that reinforce a sequential improvisation curriculum, and then teaching them in a way that empha-sizes improvisation, jazz ensemble directors maximize student learning, simultaneously benefiting the individual and the ensemble. They truly teach jazz.

THE VALUE OF MUSICAL IMPROVISATION

In today's highly scrutinized educational environment, the effective music educator must also be an informed music advocate. If we wish to build and maintain thriving music programs that include jazz, we must understand and articulate to others why music, particularly jazz improvisation, is an indispensable part of the curriculum. We need to demonstrate that, while a wealth of research indicates that music study enhances a student's achievement in other subjects, these correlations are only peripheral to the true value of music as an integral part of education and humanity.

The study of music provides distinct and important knowledge that is not gained in any other discipline. It involves unique ways of knowing that involve the whole person: physical, intellectual, and emotional.

Music, which is present in all human societies (both past and present), is an integral part of the human experience. While we do not completely understand the role of music, its omnipresence shows that it is a fundamental aspect of civilization. Students who learn music become more informed consumers of the constant barrage of musical sounds accompanying contemporary life. Through their experiences they grow to understand humanity.

Music abstractly mirrors both interactive and individualistic components of life. Through music, students experience various approaches to learning and develop new ways of thinking, a must for dealing with music's multitude of interrelated patterns. Patterns in music include the more obvious rhythmic groupings, but also highly organized levels of tension and release manifested through a complex system of interrelated elements, including time (pulse, meter, and rhythm), timbre, intensity, tonality, consonance and dissonance, and formal structures.

Musical events exist in the context and continuum of rhythmic time, producing a sequential array of action, reaction, and interaction, all progressing toward resolution. The basic element of time in music is the pulse, also known as tact, or beat. The presence of a constant pulse that is both divided (rhythm) and grouped into patterns (rhythm and meter) is unique to music. Music students must recognize and reproduce micro and macro time patterns, not only visually and cognitively, but also through aural, vocal, and kinesthetic activities. The constraint of a time continuum allows expression within constraints, creativity within a framework. It necessitates the artful discipline of performing learned skills at a specific instant.

These complex systems give students an abstract way to understand our complex and interrelated world. While students may be musical novices, they possess profound emotional abilities that enable them to *feel* deeply. In music, if not daily life, students feel conflict melt into resolution, stress negotiate with release, and tension turn to triumph. They also experience ambiguity and the interconnectedness of conflict. These sensations evoke deep personal responses as they resonate emotionally with life experiences.

Divergent emotions may be experienced (and produced) by students, including emotions that they not have previously recognized or been free to express. When music thus impacts us emotionally, it creates both immediate and lasting alterations of our emotional fabric. It changes us.

Having felt this depth of knowledge, students long retain the impressions. This may later surface in increased personal awareness, empathy, or deeper appreciation for other cultures and peoples. Involving students more actively and directly in musical performance magnifies the opportunity for aesthetic reaction.

Within these experiences, students learn both independence and interdependence (a rare thing for adolescents). Interdependence is more than mere collaboration (where levels of individual responsibility vary and true interaction is rare). In music, each individual has an integral role to play—and everyone plays. Students recognize and appreciate the value of roles divergent from their own. They learn to follow, to lead, and to merge from many into one.

Add this to the emotional impact that music can convey, and the performance of music truly involves the whole student as no other discipline can. They constantly perform, experience, create, and feel, moving far beyond the level of passive participants to a place of intrapersonal and interpersonal insight. While the meaning of musical messages may differ from student to student, each learns in a way that is not only mental and physical, but also emotional, intuitive, and personal—fully human.

Successful improvisation heightens the efficacy of the musical experience. It allows students to directly create, rather than re-create, meaning. In improvisation, victory springs not only from past training, but also from immediate personal choices. Students learn to recognize different ways of resolving a situation, to search for better solutions.

Improvised music differs from written composition in another important way as well. Improvisations never become a finished product, even though they may be perceived as a cohesive or complete unit of music. They are "ongoing activity rather than sculpted time" (Day, 2000, p. 105). Improvised music expresses fluid moments, sometimes related to things previous or subsequent, but just as often singular. Improvisation speaks directly to the ambiguity of the human experience, to our continually shifting awareness and perceptions. It contains, even more so than written music, the opportunity for failure juxtaposed with the thrill of creation. Improvisation represents knowing and acting *in the moment*.

The ability to improvise is as universal as the ability to enjoy music, though not as frequently nurtured. The close correlation between musical improvisation and inherent aspects of human development and interaction may partly explain why improvisation has such emotional potency.

The gentle music-like communications of mother to infant imbue our first aural interaction with a spontaneous musical context. Within this context of musical-sound-as-communication, infants learn to react and elicit reactions, both as "turn taking" and "synchronous interaction." A major step in the development of communication occurs when "infants develop an understanding of intentionality—that they can affect others in a predictable way" (Perry, 2003, p. 228). These early experiences teach communication-through-music as unplanned interaction.

The first music children create is improvisatory. The stage of child development known as "spontaneous song" usually occurs around age two as children experiment vocally with music and sounds to play and express themselves (Radocy & Boyle, 2003).

The presence of learned elements differentiates refined musical improvisation from spontaneous song. "Improvisation is not the same as spontaneous musicking. Rehearsal appears to be a necessary prior condition for such improvisation because it allows a growing mastery of elements that can be combined in novel ways for that individual" (Welch, 1999, p. 214). It is important to note that while the *inclination* to improvise is universal, the *ability* to improvise musically must be attained through "rehearsal." In reality, both adult improvisation and children's spontaneous song combine known musical materials in new and meaningful ways. Both types of improvisation express meaning and emotion through music; the difference lies mainly in the complexity of the material and the restraint of the context.

Children gradually incorporate learned songs into their improvisations. Often, learned songs completely replace spontaneous creations. With encouragement, children can continue to experiment with spontaneous music while learning other musical elements. This scenario nurtures personal expression, while preparing children to create more refined improvisations, such as those used in jazz.

Older children also seem naturally inclined to improvise. Kanellopoulos (1999) studied eight-year-old children placed in an environment filled with musical instruments. Without prior instruction or musical training, the children developed an organized and expressive system of musical improvisation. They verbally expressed a desire to communicate emotions and ideas through their improvised music. When they felt they had succeeded in this, the children expressed satisfaction and happiness.

Even simplistic improvisations serve an aesthetic function for the participants. Improvisation offers aesthetic involvement on individual terms, regardless of musical finesse. It allows children to *discover* successful roles as they find ways to express deep musical and personal meaning. Children not inclined to express emotion overtly may find expression and emotional fulfillment through musical performance, especially improvisatory performance.

These connections between musical improvisation and human emotion and communication are further evidenced by the use of improvisation in the field of music therapy. In music therapy (MT) improvisation, music making becomes a tool for therapeutic progress. MT improvisation succeeds in a wide variety of therapeutic applications because music, specifically improvised music, connects intimately with the way humans feel and communicate.

Perry (2003) identified an important similarity between verbal communication and music improvisation. "One aspect of communication that has sometimes been neglected is its reciprocal, dynamic, and active nature. Each communication partner affects the other, and the outcome and forms of communication are not predetermined, or controlled by one partner. This theme is also prominent in descriptions of improvisational music therapy" (p. 230).

After noting similarities between improvisation and communication, Pavlicevic (2000) concludes that "MT improvisation is human communication in sound: it is a direct communicating and experiencing of one-self through the elements of tempo, rhythm, contour, shape, motion, and texture of music, speech, vocalizing, gestures, and facial expression. We experience these elements in MT improvisation not only as musical, but also as personal, and relational" (p. 275).

The success of MT improvisation across a multitude of personalities and conditions suggests that all humans (excepting some of the severely disabled) can improvise personally meaningful music when given the opportunity. MT improvisation research also shows that improvisation can reveal inner emotional experiences and reflect the way we view the world (Smeijsters & van den Hurk, 1999).

Improvisation constitutes the original element in the musical evolution of all societies. Even today, most indigenous and folk music styles retain improvised elements. Some, such as ragas and flamenco, operate according to well-developed and complex patterns of improvisation. Western societies also integrated improvisation as an essential aspect of musical performance until the end of the baroque era. Even during the classical era, large formal structures often included improvisational opportunities, as in the cadenza of a concerto. Significantly, many renowned composers, including Handel, Bach, Mozart, and Beethoven, were also noted improvisers.

In contemporary times, improvisatory musical styles flourish mainly *outside* of the classical tradition. Improvisational genres seem uniquely suited to express the feelings of the disenfranchised; perhaps new genres develop when listeners do not relate emotionally to existing institutionalized music styles. Spirituals, blues, work songs, jazz in its many forms, and rap all have origins in improvisation. In recent years the "turntablism" of DJs scratching and spinning records has exploded in popularity as a new improvisational genre.

The continual resurgence of improvisation is an intriguing indicator of a universal desire to create personally expressive music. This is just one example of how music, including jazz improvisation, provides a lens through which we better understand the personal motivations that drive society's history, hardships, and triumphs.

In truth, all musicians improvise. While improvisation as the spontaneous creation of new melodies is easily recognizable, forms of improvisation also occur when performers interpret or alter written music. Additionally, the urge to create manifests itself in less conventional ways: experiments with unusual sounds or unconventional performance techniques, concocting new lyrics to existing melodies, altering or exaggerating musical elements, creating humor by performing in an intentionally extreme way, and so forth. All of this approaches improvisation, for in these moments we use *what we know* to act *as we feel*.

Beyond these lofty ideals, jazz directors reap a more pragmatic benefit from teaching improvisation. "Knowledge of improvisation is an absolute necessity if one is to do a first class job anywhere in a jazz band. Knowing something of improvisation is bound to provide insights that will improve the quality of the student's playing" (Baker, 1988, v).

The National Standards for Music Education (National Arts Education Association, 1994) recognize the need to include improvisation in a comprehensive music education. Improvisation is a primary method of instruction in elementary music classrooms, but tends to receive less attention in secondary schools. Since the format for most secondary music classes is the large performing ensemble, the instructional emphasis often shifts from promoting individual discovery to perfecting group performance. There, an individual performer's personal choices are limited in favor of actions prescribed by the composer or director. Especially in the case of the jazz ensemble, the goals of individual and group expression ought not be divergent.

Improvisation constitutes one of the defining characteristics of jazz. Throughout the development of jazz, improvisation has been both an essential aspect of professional performance and a vehicle for learning jazz style. To use knowledge instantly in improvisation requires that the musical "raw materials" be deeply learned, not just superficially understood. Students must gain the technical skills that enable them to address all of the elements of music, including harmony, phrase structure, melodic development, and musical interaction. They must develop true personal musicianship.

Still, eliciting value in improvisation isn't easy. Sporadic and superficial activities only familiarize students with improvisational contexts (forms and styles). Students must be provided with sufficient time and opportunity in order to transcend context and move toward truly meaningful improvisation. At the same time, students look forward to performing and may have limited patience for activities that seem, to them, unrelated to the upcoming concert.

By better understanding the nature of improvisation (the process by which it is accomplished), we can identify instructional strategies that are both effective and meaningful for students and avoid those practices that provide no real nourishment.

THE NATURE OF MUSICAL IMPROVISATION

An understanding of the process of improvisation illuminates the importance of effective improvisation instruction. Research suggests that improvisation involves a two-stage mental process to first generate and then evaluate musical ideas (Johnson-Laird, 2002). The generative stage occurs in long-term memory and may be understood as subconscious thoughts based upon the residue of prior experiences. The evaluative stage occurs in short-term ("working") memory and involves conscious thought and decision. At the time of creation, musical materials are subconsciously presented by the generative stage. The improviser then consciously chooses and performs material.

"The bottleneck in improvisation, as in cognition in general, is the limited processing capacity of working memory" (Johnson-Laird, 2002, p. 442). By nature, the generative stage simply accepts everything it encounters. It later presents to the evaluative stage those things that have become most indelible.

The generative stage is most effective when only useful musical materials (scales, melodies, rhythms, articulation patterns, etc.) have been ingrained. To accomplish this, learning experiences are guided by constraints. Limiting and refining the generative possibilities reduces the cognitive load, thereby increasing the speed of generation. Simpler improvisational formats (e.g., simple scale types, limited changes in harmony) also enable beginners to experience meaningful improvisation by reducing the amount of material they must consciously consider. As students grow in experience and skill, more materials become ingrained and their capabilities expand.

Each improvisational experience affects subsequent experiences. Materials learned deliberately eventually spring to mind automatically. By introducing materials carefully and sequentially, teachers can ensure that only acceptable (stylistically and harmonically correct) materials become ingrained in long-term memory. Ideally, then, *only* productive choices come to the student-improviser's mind in the moment of performance. As these ideas present themselves for conscious evaluation, an appropriate idea is selected and quickly performed.

Musicians using unfamiliar musical materials (scales, chords, rhythms, etc.) to improvise must operate exclusively from conscious, evaluative thought. Although some aurally gifted individuals may intuitively respond with musical improvisations, the majority of improvisers are presented with the impossibility of creating melodic improvisations while simultaneously consciously considering shifting scale/chord choices, phrase structure, and form. When novice improvisers encounter such unwieldy challenges in jazz ensemble literature, they are likely to ignore important requirements (such as adhering to the harmonic structure) and to become discouraged.

David Baker uses an effective analogy to illustrate the difficulty of improvising with novel materials: "While the results are less damaging physically, the jazz musician without a repository of patterns, licks, etc., is in a position quite similar to a boxer who must think about every punch he throws, instead of automatically reacting to a given situation with firmly implanted combinations based on empirical data" (1989, p. 4).

Beginning improvisers need significant rehearsal opportunities in order to master musical materials. For instance, musicians must rehearse the same scale pattern many times before it becomes ingrained to the degree that it can be played with little conscious effort. Again, one is reminded that "Rehearsal appears to be a necessary prior condition for . . . improvisation because it allows a growing mastery of elements that can be combined in novel ways for that individual" (Welch, 1999, p. 214).

Much of improvisation is based upon material that the performer deliberately rehearses prior to the performance. "Improvisation does not mean that 'anything goes,' or that everything a performer comes up with will be completely new and original" (Sawyer, 1999, p. 194).

What generative materials should be learned, and in what way are they limited? Identifying two structural levels for improvisation illuminates the types of materials that improvisers deal with. Improvisation is made up primarily of (1) melodic building blocks (scales and melodic licks), and (2) the "global structures" of form and genre (Sawyer, 1999, p. 197). These structural levels can also be described more simply as "The things that hold a solo together . . . the use of simple motifs and the repeating harmonic sequence of the theme" (Johnson-Laird, 2002, p. 432).

David Baker differentiates between fixed parameters (such as form, meter, and harmonic structure) and flexible parameters (such as articulation, dynamics, vibrato, and rhythm) that improvisers must address (2003, p. 4). He also suggests that "Playing the correct chord changes/proper scales, retaining the form, keeping the tempo and swinging ought to be givens and should be the barest minimum demanded of a good soloist" (1997, p. 63).

Although many people recognize that these concerns must be addressed by a "good soloist," fewer consider that the same concerns should direct beginning improvisation. Some simple experiences can lay the groundwork for later success in these areas. "Improvisational skill begins with some important activities: listening to improvised music, learning a repertoire by ear, understanding harmonic progression, and taking the risks necessary to improvise" (Azzara, 1999, p. 22).

One of the most unwieldy challenges for young improvisers involves merely keeping the correct place in the progressing harmonies of the form. "Many students begin improvising a solo only to stop in frustration because they are lost. They do not know where they are in the structure of the tune. This may be partially caused by the inability to 'hear' the chord changes, but it is largely due to inability to conceive the passage of rhythmic time as it is related to the composition being performed" (Kynaston & Ricci, 1978, p. 4).

Students must have many improvisational experiences in order to move beyond familiarity and to truly memorize and internalize materials, including jazz forms (harmonic progressions). The rehearsal of jazz ensemble charts that include improvisation provides a promising format for such experiences, despite the significant challenges inherent in this approach.

CONCLUSION

Improvised music provides students meaningful intellectual and aesthetic experiences that cannot be realized in any other way. Successful improvisation experiences prepare students for a world of increasing ambiguity by enabling them to confront and transcend uncertainty. Perhaps most importantly, students who improvise are constantly aware of the preeminent goal of music—to perform in a way that elicits aesthetic feeling from performer and audience.

Music educators who understand the nature of improvisation make better-informed choices about the curricular materials (including jazz ensemble charts) and instructional methods they use to maximize student success.

2

THE EVOLUTION OF
JAZZ IN EDUCATION

The ever-burgeoning market of books, magazines, CDs, DVDs, audio downloads, podcasts, and websites dedicated to jazz and jazz education could lead us to conclude that the current state of things in jazz education is a finished product, carefully designed and meticulously implemented.

Hardly.

In many ways the continuing evolution of jazz education mirrors the messy cross-pollination that cultivated jazz itself. Jazz did not originate from conservatories, scholarly treatises, or committee recommendations. It is a child of mixed parentage. A formative amalgam of blues, spirituals, hymns, marches, Spanish influences, and classical music gave rise to the style, but there is more to the story. The potent formative friction of divergent cultures in a convergent society included not only elements of music and race but also the more earthy concerns of economics. After all, a musician has to make a living.

Likewise, while jazz education owes much to the artistry and intellect of visionary musician-educators, current practices also bear the brand of past and present commercialism. For example, the "standard instrumentation" of today's jazz ensembles stems, not from research regarding ideal learning environments, but from the type of charts commercial music publishers chose to produce in the middle of the last century. This does not diminish the artistic or educational merit of the jazz ensemble, but illustrates the level of influence commercial entities have historically wielded on jazz education.

Consider the reality that the bulk of the jazz ensemble curriculum (the charts) continues to come, not from professional educators, but from professional musicians, and you've identified a wildcard that imbues educational jazz with virility and relevance, but that also presents some thorny challenges.

A brief overview of the evolution of formal jazz education shows that, while current practices are increasingly informed by research and sound pedagogy, they remain inescapably rooted to past exigencies.

ORIGINS

Common wisdom once held that no one could be taught jazz; that playing the style, specifically the ability to improvise, required an innate talent, a mystical gift.

Or, to take the opposite view, a curse.

Most classically trained musicians initially viewed jazz with contempt. Perhaps this was due to racism, musical snobbery, or simply the association of jazz music with questionable performance venues. Regardless, jazz was not welcome in polite society, much less the classroom.

Jazz originated in an informal environment, relying more upon popular tastes, folk styles, musical coalescence, and experimentation than upon tradition and rigid pedagogy. Listening to and mimicking the music of established jazz performers became the first and best teacher of the style. While formal instruction was scarce in the first decades of the twentieth century, a lot of learning went on, partly in the form of "on-the-job training" in working bands. Older musicians served as mentors, or at least as role models, to aspiring musicians. (This continues to be an excellent way to learn jazz.) Emulating the masters by ear became increasingly valuable as improvisation became a defining characteristic of jazz.

That many purveyors of the new style could not read notated music was evidence enough for those who could that the music itself was somehow inferior. A peculiar type of reverse musical discrimination developed in tandem: some jazz musicians held that learning to read music would ruin a person's ability to play jazz. Little wonder then that school music teachers trained in the classical style would be disinclined to teach the style.

Still, even early on, jazz education had a few forward-looking pioneers.

EDUCATIONAL FOUNDATIONS

Because blues inflections and forms infuse all styles of jazz, blues giant William C. Handy must also be considered a forerunner of jazz education. He became one of the first blues or jazz musicians to receive formal training when he studied music with Y. A. Wallace of Fisk University. Then, around 1900, Handy taught at the Teacher's Agricultural and Mechanical College for Negroes. It is natural to suppose that Handy taught his students blues as well as classical music; however, no specific information regarding his teaching methods has survived. By 1907 Handy had relocated to Memphis, where he actively taught the blues style. In addition to his educational contributions, Handy composed many blues tunes that continue to influence today's blues and jazz musicians.

Ragtime, or "syncopated," music provided much of the basis for jazz's swing rhythms. A common performance practice around the turn of the century was to play existing musical arrangements with alterations to the rhythm (changing even eighth notes into dotted-eighth/sixteenth combinations). The resulting ragged, or syncopated, rhythm probably gave ragtime its name. While today's audiences are most familiar with ragtime music for piano, many working bands and orchestras also performed the music.

James Reese Europe, renowned as a bandleader, must also be acknowledged as an early educator in the developing jazz art form. Europe's groups enjoyed so much success performing syncopated music in New York City that, in 1910, he formed a black musician's union to promote and perform the music. Europe offered all members of the union instruction in performing and composing music in the syncopated style.

Possibly the first conventional instruction in jazz came from Len Bowden. From 1919 to 1945, Bowden trained musicians and helped form bands at institutions, including Tuskegee Institute, Georgia State College, Alabama State Normal College, and Great Lakes Navy Base. Even in his early teaching, Bowden included jazz instruction in the areas of improvisation, arranging, composition, and rehearsal techniques.

The advent of recording technology in 1917 expanded the influence of jazz tremendously by exposing musicians in all parts of the country to the music. This technology, probably more than any single person, prompted the learning of jazz. Irrespective of the supposed impossibility of teaching jazz, once they could hear it, countless musicians were driven to learn the style on their own.

1920s

With few teachers offering jazz instruction and no jazz instructional or method books, most aspiring jazz musicians of the 1920s learned jazz aurally, through live performances, radio, and records. Jazz was generally viewed as novelty music with dubious social value and little academic merit. Notwithstanding the instances already mentioned, formal jazz instruction was rare. Still, unlike the majority of their contemporaries who viewed jazz improvisation with either disdain or a certain unapproachable awe, a handful of classically trained musicians had now begun to perform in the new style.

As the 1920s drew to a close, the small "traditional" or "Dixieland" groups that relied heavily on collective improvisation began to be supplanted by larger ensembles performing from written arrangements. Some of these arrangements became commercially available. Designed for dancing, they rarely included any improvisation opportunities (Wiskirchen, 1975). The presence of written arrangements allowed musicians to participate in jazz performance without learning to improvise.

Although variations in instrumentation would continue for some time, the instrumentation of many jazz ensembles began to be determined by the printed music, rather than the inverse. By publishing music for a predetermined instrumentation, publishers played a pivotal role in shaping the type of ensemble that would later become the core of educational jazz programs.

1930s

In the 1930s jazz emerged as a dominant force in American popular music. In large urban areas, increasing numbers of private teachers focused solely on jazz instruction. New resources also fed the burgeoning public interest in jazz; *Downbeat* magazine's first jazz column began in 1935. Popular jazz performers published instructional books, sometimes including play-along records. Doron Antrim's 1936 book *Secrets of Dance Band Success* featured essays by popular bandleaders, including Jimmy Dorsey and Duke Ellington.

Still, many classically trained musicians disdained jazz, banning it from college music buildings and practice rooms. While jazz had little formal presence in academia, students still learned the music outside of the classroom. Campuses were often home to student-run "dance bands." (Because the term "jazz" suffered from a salacious connotation, most high school and college jazz ensembles identified themselves instead as dance bands, and later as stage bands or swing bands.) Les Brown led such a group at Duke University before attaining musical fame.

In 1928 Joseph Schillinger came to the United States and subsequently began teaching an innovative system of composition that influenced many jazz musicians. Schillinger taught at various New York–area universities in the 1930s and carried on an extensive correspondence course. His students included Glenn Miller and George Gershwin. Schillinger's principles formed the core curriculum of Schillinger House, founded in 1945—known today as the Berklee College of Music.

1940s

The greatest growth in jazz instruction during the 1940s came not to colleges, but to high schools, where stage bands enjoyed immense popularity. The sudden advent of secondary school jazz ensemble classes in the 1940s may be partly attributed to the desire to preserve community music making in the absence of older musicians who were now involved in military duty. Most school ensembles focused on dance music, with little improvisation—a reflection of the type of charts available at the time. Few music educators had any experience with jazz improvisation.

During World War II, the number of musicians employed by the U.S. military (primarily performing swing music) increased greatly. Recognizing the popularity of jazz, the U.S. Navy Music Academy Training School began offering formal instruction in jazz performance and arranging before any civilian colleges were doing so. The military purchased musical instruments en masse, helping to build a thriving instrument-manufacturing industry.

With the end of the war, the musical-instrument industry faced drastic reductions in the military market for their instruments. Focusing their attention on secondary schools, the industry successfully promoted instrumental music programs, leading to the continued growth of band and stage band programs.

The number of available music teachers also increased, as the GI Bill supported an influx of trained military musicians into colleges. Their previous jazz experience affected both the college programs they participated in and the bands they would later teach.

In the 1940s, Alabama State, Tennessee State, Wilberforce University, Westlake College of Music, Berklee College of Music, Los Angeles City College, and North Texas State College began to offer jazz courses for credit. (There is some debate as to which college first offered a jazz course for credit, but the general consensus points to North Texas State College in 1943.) Other colleges also began to include jazz through non-credit courses or extracurricular ensembles.

Serious jazz scholarship developed during the 1940s as scholars, including influential jazz critic Leonard Feather, began presenting college lectures on the history of jazz.

1950s

Several events significantly improved the overall quality of jazz education during the 1950s. Former military musicians with jazz performance experience entered the teaching profession, making this the first generation of students with a chance of being taught authentic jazz style in secondary school. Additional training came through summer jazz instruction programs that brought professional musicians into contact with educators and students. Two such programs were Indiana University's National Stage Band Camp and Marshall Stearn's Jazz in the Summer seminars. Excepting a few localized pockets of excellence, most school jazz programs focused on ensemble performance rather than jazz improvisation.

While dance-oriented arrangements were available, printed music appropriate for school stage bands was difficult to obtain. Educators often wrote arrangements themselves or hand-copied professional arrangements when touring jazz bands visited their area. Then, in 1954, a singular event occurred. Jazz musician and educator Art Dedrick, working with partners in the newly formed Kendor Music, arranged and distributed music designed specifically for the school stage band; the songs were the first to be published expressly for school stage bands.

In the years that followed, a flood of music published for stage band would solidify standardized instrumentation and provide ample teaching material for high school and college jazz ensemble courses. The charts became the curriculum. With a steady source of music now available, high school and college stage bands became increasingly common. By the end of the decade, approximately forty colleges and five thousand high schools in the United States offered at least one jazz course, usually stage band.

Further evidence that jazz was entering the mainstream came as the Music Educators National Conference (MENC: The National Association for Music Education) invited jazz artists, including Dave Brubeck, to perform at the organization's 1958 conference.

1960s

Although the commercial popularity of jazz music declined during the 1960s, jazz education increased dramatically. The first college jazz degrees were developed at North Texas State, Indiana University, Millikan University, the University of Illinois, Berklee College of Music, Southern University, and Los Angeles City College.

The educators who pioneered this development were among the first of a new generation—exemplary jazz musicians who had also attained the academic credentials requisite for employment in higher education. They included Buddy Baker, David Baker, Alvin Batiste, Lawrence Berk, Leon Breeden, Jerry Coker, Gene Hall, Bob McDonald, Roger Schueler, and Bob Share. Another, John LaPorta, contributed one of the first books on teaching jazz in schools, *Developing the School Jazz Ensemble*, in 1965. (An even earlier handling of the topic was George Wiskirchen's book *Developmental Techniques for the School Dance Band* , published in 1961.) As in the secondary schools, the large jazz ensemble was usually the centerpiece of a university's jazz program.

Collegiate jazz festivals grew in number from twelve in 1960 to seventy-five in 1969. These festivals typically focused on competition between jazz ensembles. By the end of the decade, approximately three hundred colleges and ten thousand high schools offered at least one jazz course. In the majority of schools, the focus remained the rehearsal of a large jazz ensemble, and the curriculum consisted mainly of commercially produced charts.

M. E. Hall's 1961 book *Teacher's Guide to the High School Stage Band* reflects the emphasis of many secondary school jazz programs of the time. The brief text focuses entirely on the correct interpretation of the written page, noting only that improvisation "is usually beyond the abilities of most high school students" (p. 1).

While improvisation may not have been foremost in the minds of many school band directors, professional jazz musicians became increasingly interested in sharing their knowledge with students. Many became involved in education, giving workshops and contributing to the publication of jazz charts and other materials. Jerry Coker's *Improvising Jazz*, published in 1964, presented one of the first written treatises addressing the harmonic and stylistic demands of jazz improvisation. One of the first jazz patterns books, Oliver Nelson's *Patterns for Improvisation*, was published in 1966. Jamey Aebersold's seminal Play-A-Long series began in 1967 with the publication of *How to Play Jazz and Improvise*. His books (now numbering well over one hundred volumes) allowed aspiring improvisers to practice improvisation along with recordings of professional rhythm sections.

It is significant to note a somewhat divergent approach that began at this time and persists even today: the bulk of improvisational materials were aimed at individual musicians, while written music (with minimal improvisation opportunities) was being used as the primary curriculum of the jazz ensemble.

Even as jazz waned as popular music, its increasing recognition as legitimate art music prompted continued growth in academia. As the civil rights movement focused attention on African American culture and contributions, some colleges established departments of African American Studies that included jazz study. The 1967 Symposium on Youth Music at Tanglewood, Massachusetts, called for the further growth of jazz in education. Part of that growth included the formation of the National Association for Jazz Educators (NAJE) in 1968 as an affiliate of MENC: The National Association for Music Education.

David Baker, who had already written extensively about jazz and improvisation, penned one such guide in 1969, a book entitled *David Baker's Jazz Pedagogy: A Comprehensive Method of Jazz Education for Teacher and Student.*

1970s

In 1973, the NAJE held its first national convention. The workshops targeted both educators and professional performers; since its inception, NAJE has attempted to involve professional jazz musicians with the professional educators that make up the bulk of its membership.

Around 170 collegiate jazz festivals occurred annually in the 1970s, with the emphasis gradually shifting toward a noncompetitive format.

Most young people who learned anything about jazz now did so because of their membership in a school jazz ensemble. While the curricular resources created specifically for jazz ensemble still consisted almost exclusively of written charts, educators found ways to adapt instructional texts, personal know-how, and play-along books in order to teach jazz history, theory, and improvisation.

Transcription books are another type of resource that offer insight into the art of improvisation. These books consist of notated versions of improvised solos by the masters of jazz. One of the first collections, the *Charlie Parker Omnibook*, transcribed by Jamey Aebersold and Ken Slone, was published in 1978 and has been a perennial favorite ever since.

Improvisation books, such as the 1970 *Patterns for Jazz*, by Jerry Coker, James Casale, Gary Campbell, and Jerry Greene, and the 1978 *Jazz Improvisation*, by Trent Kynaston and Robert Ricci, now routinely included not only theoretical explanations, but also extensive collections of notated jazz patterns to play over various harmonic progressions.

A growing awareness of the distinct expertise needed to successfully teach jazz in secondary schools resulted in a new resources aimed at that audience.

1980s

Some modest attempts at collaborative jazz curriculum development were suggested in the 1980s. NAJE's chairman of the National K–12 Curriculum Committee, Rick Arnold, began a series of articles in the *Jazz Educators Journal* in 1981. He intended to present curriculum suggestions as part of the development of a national jazz curriculum. (To date, no such curriculum has been completed.)

Additional teacher resources, such as Richard Lawn's *The Jazz Ensemble Director's Manual* (1981), and John Kuzmich and Lee Bash's *Complete Guide to Instrumental Jazz Instruction* (1984) provided educators who may not have received any previous jazz training with information, resources, and techniques to help them teach jazz ensemble.

Publishers, having become aware of the difficulty educators encountered in teaching improvisation, increasingly included optional written solos in their charts as an alternative to improvisation. Whatever the motivation for it, this practice led many to overuse notated solos at the expense of teaching improvisation. Students could easily be part of a jazz ensemble for years without learning anything about improvisation.

Many college jazz education programs began including aspects of popular and commercial music instruction. This trend was echoed in the publishing world as an increasing amount of popular music was published for jazz ensemble.

In 1988 PG Music released a computer software program called Band-in-a-Box. This software allowed users to input chord symbols that could then be played back in the form of a midi accompaniment. Along with other features, the software provided the flexibility to quickly create and practice with the harmonic background for any song.

In 1989 the name of the NAJE was changed to its current form: International Association for Jazz Education (IAJE). The name change reflected an effort to involve jazz educators from around the globe in preserving, promoting, and improving jazz education.

In the same year, the Thelonious Monk Institute formed to offer resources, curriculum, and scholarships in jazz. One goal of the organization is the development of a national K–12 jazz curriculum. Interestingly, the organization has not targeted its curriculum toward the jazz ensemble. Rather, instruction is chiefly intended for social studies or history classes and focuses on understanding and appreciating jazz, not on performance. Resources and curriculum plans were initially launched in 2000. Eventually materials, including visual and audio resources, lesson plans, and assessments, became available for use in fifth-, eighth-, and eleventh-grade classrooms.

1990s

College jazz programs continued to attain greater esteem in the 1990s. In more and more cases, the gap between the professional performer and the professional educator disappeared, with prominent jazz performers also holding advanced degrees and faculty positions. More programs offered a breadth of courses including jazz history, theory, composition and arranging, pedagogy, improvisation, research, and alternative performance ensembles. Graduate degree programs in jazz began to develop at many schools.

The progress of college jazz programs benefited secondary schools as well. School band directors in the 1990s were more likely than ever to have received a college jazz education themselves. Despite this improvement, the vast majority of music education majors (those who would later become the teachers of secondary school jazz ensembles) were not required to participate in *any* jazz training prior to graduation.

Perhaps spurred on by the inclusion of improvisation in the National Standards for Music Education, the publishers of classroom method books for bands and orchestras began to address the need for similar materials for the jazz band. The first of these full-class methods, the *Standard of Excellence Jazz Ensemble Method*, was published in 1998.

The same year, Shelly Berg's *Chop-Monster Jazz Language Tutor* books also became available. These books are also designed specifically for use in the jazz ensemble rehearsal, but focus exclusively on jazz improvisation. The accompanying compact discs contain a sequence of aural exercises and jazz call-and-response patterns. Like the *Standard of*

Excellence Jazz Ensemble Method, the *Chop-Monster* book includes charts so that full-band performances can be integrated with improvisation instruction.

The advent of the Internet and innovations in music technology may eventually prove to be as influential to jazz as was the invention of recording technology at the dawn of the jazz age. Software to aid improvisation, such as Band-in-a-Box, Smartmusic, and MiBAC Jazz, continually improved, and a multitude of other pedagogical aids became available.

The Second Century

Current membership in IAJE is over eight thousand, with members in forty-two countries. Annual international conferences are supplemented by regional teacher-training institutes. Other professional organizations, including MENC: The National Association for Music Education, also provide jazz resources and training.

Well over one hundred American colleges now offer an undergraduate degree in jazz. Jazz graduate degrees are becoming more and more common, including a small number of doctoral programs. Although elective jazz courses are now available at most institutions of higher education, it remains uncommon for universities to make jazz training a required part of a music education degree.

In 2004, a British organization, the Associated Board of the Royal School of Music (ABRSM), introduced a sequential jazz curriculum that includes some material for large jazz ensemble. (Portions of the curriculum have been used outside the United States for some time, but could not be sold domestically due to copyright restrictions.) This material comprises the most complete jazz curriculum to date and includes sequential, performance-based instruction and evaluation for jazz and jazz improvisation. The fact that this important milestone occurred outside of the United States indicates the scope of jazz's influence and may foreshadow future developments.

The availability of music and information via the Internet continues to grow exponentially. Online audio, master classes, blogs, videos, and interactive lessons offer a wealth of opportunities for students of jazz.

As methods and materials proliferate, the evolution of jazz education continues. In the past, the scarcity of curricular materials made it necessary for jazz educators to forge their own routes in teaching improvisation. Today's jazz educators may find themselves similarly disoriented by the opposite condition. The sheer volume of material now available forces educators to navigate a confusingly cluttered path.

Since jazz ensemble charts still constitute the *primary* curriculum for most jazz education programs, two preeminent tasks remain: choosing charts that best suit the needs of the students, and teaching the charts in a way that maximizes the usefulness of their content.

3

WHAT IS SUCCESSFUL
IMPROVISATION?

What is successful improvisation? This is a wonderfully dangerous question. It is akin to asking, What is successful music? Intriguing fodder for a graduate-level philosophy discussion, but impossible to answer definitively.

Still, without recognizable indicators of success, how can we properly focus our teaching? For the purpose of teaching jazz improvisation (the focus of this book), successful improvisation is defined rather narrowly as improvisation that exhibits the characteristic elements of the common practice styles of jazz performance. By gaining a better understanding of the component parts of improvisation, we illuminate the path to improved instruction and assessment.

All students in the jazz ensemble should be taught to master these elements of improvisation.

ELEMENTS OF IMPROVISATION

Following are many of the characteristics (surely not all) that contribute to a successful improvised solo. Each element must be deeply ingrained in order to be accessible to the student in an improvisation situation.

Musical Fundamentals

Improvisations should be, above all else, musical. Considerations of proper tone and intonation, playing position, and (where applicable) air support cannot be overemphasized. The best way to prepare jazz students for nuances of articulation, timbre, and flexibility of pitch is for the director to insist on the same fundamental tone quality and technique that ensure success to the concert band. The challenges of improvisation make it all the more important for students to make use of the musical skills they have previously attained.

Pulse and Meter

The improviser plays in a way that is connected to, and consistent with, the pulse of a song. The improvisation also demonstrates an awareness of meter and of the strong and weak beats within each measure. (This may seem an obvious statement, but those who work with young musicians, especially young improvisers, know that playing exactly on time is an ongoing challenge.)

Internal Rhythm

The improviser's eighth notes consistently exhibit the correct subdivision of the beat, either into straight eighth notes (as found in most rock and Latin styles) or swing eighth notes. This rhythmic awareness is evidenced both in the subdivisions of the beat and when grouping those subdivisions with longer notes. The development of a convincing swing style is an absolute must for all aspiring jazz improvisers, as swing eighth notes are a predominate element in most jazz solos.

Articulation

The soloist's articulation is appropriate for the style being played. Articulation is inseparably connected with proper swing style. Swing articulation can generally be described as legato, but with dramatic accents, including tongue cut-offs. Articulation should serve to accentuate the important notes of the phrase. Excessive or unnaturally exaggerated tonguing or scooping quickly destroys the correct style and are to be avoided.

Correct Style

When the subdivisions of the beat (swing or straight) and the articulation are performed correctly, the overall style of the solo likely fits with the style of the song being played. Because nuances in style vary from performer to performer, students should listen to great jazz recordings as much as possible in order to begin recognizing these differences. Significant differences, for instance, are noticeable between the performance styles of Glenn Miller and Tito Puente.

Rhythmic Interest

The rhythms used in improvisation exhibit a balance of unity and variety that makes the music expressive and unpredictable, but not unintelligible. Rhythms are developed through use of repetition with variation.

Note Choice

The pitches played by the soloist should continually correspond with the changing harmonies of the song. When the chord changes, the improviser reflects the change by playing a significant note (usually a chord tone) of the new chord. Dissonances are acceptable when they resolve appropriately or contribute to the overall shape and effectiveness of the solo.

Solo Development

The improviser's musical ideas regularly have relation to not only the underlying harmony but also, in some discernable way, the other musical elements, whether they be from the song's melody, the playing of accompanying instruments, or previous and subsequent material played by the soloist. The effect of solo development is the production of musical ideas that engage the listener. An effective solo mixes elements of cohesiveness, or unity, with novel elements to create variety.

Space

Compelling solos contain not only notes but also meaningful rests. These pauses give the audience time to absorb the material, promote phrase structure, and provide opportunities for the rhythm section to interact without becoming overbearing. Rests also give the soloist time to reflect, listen, and prepare to play again.

Interaction

Effective soloists and rhythm sections communicate with one another, for instance, by adjusting their playing to compliment each other. This may be accomplished through aural and occasional visual cues between the soloist and accompanying instruments. Interaction also refers to the way the soloist plays to the audience with confidence and appropriate stage presence.

Melody and Phrasing

Using appropriate note choices and a variety of rhythmic material, improvisers produce complete phrases that are cohesive and melodic. Notes must in some way combine into groups. The length and complexity of successful phrases vary greatly among master improvisers. If a song being studied has lyrics, learning them, singing them, and listening to reference recordings can tremendously improve phrasing in both the melody and improvised portions of the song.

Dynamics

Dynamic change enhances the emotional impact of an improvised solo. Dynamics change to promote interaction, reflect phrase structure, and match the mood and orchestration of the accompanying instruments. Music ought not to be a language where one is constantly shouting.

Special Effects

Jazz musicians sometimes modify their tone through the use of mutes or specialized techniques such as subtone, growling, flutter-tonguing, half-valve playing, and the like. If employed during improvisation, these should be done in a way that adds to, and doesn't detract from, the overall effectiveness of the solo.

Overall Shape

Shape, or contour, refers to the ebb and flow of intensity over the course of an entire solo that forms an overall structure. It may be compared to a musical journey, wherein each phrase is one leg of the route. Improvised solos commonly build intensity and dynamics from their beginning to a point near the end.

By choosing harmonically appropriate notes and using phrasing and dynamics to build an appropriate contour, students show that they are aware of, and able to express, the moments of tension and release innately present in the harmony of the song. An effective overall contour can give a solo a sense of cohesiveness even in the absence of other recognizable methods of development, because all of the material fits within a discernable shape.

Creativity

A musical act does not need to be novel to be considered creative. Because creativity is, by definition, the motivating force behind any intentional act of creation, all improvisation is innately creative. Creativity is enhanced when improvisers make musical choices that are new for them, notwithstanding that the musical elements they use may be familiar. Students' improvisations should ultimately demonstrate the ability to perform learned elements in original incarnations, thus creating new musical material.

Emotional Impact

The successful solo has emotional resonance with the performer, the other musicians, and the audience. Although difficult to quantify, this is the entire purpose of all of the aforementioned items.

This list is long, but that is no reason for discouragement. Obviously, it would be inappropriate to expect artist-quality improvisation of a beginning improviser, but we can and should expect mastery of the simpler subsets that lead to artistic improvisation. The instructor must determine acceptable standards of performance at each level of training, from novice to advanced, and then institute a plan to lead students along that continuum. Consider also that in our increasingly assessment-driven educational environment, an additional reason to identify success is so that it can be objectively measured.

4

LIMITATIONS OF CURRENT RESOURCES AND PRACTICES

Jazz pedagogy is still in its infancy. Professional practice and scholarly research now suggest effective educational methods, but current resources do not yet fully facilitate these approaches.

Today the vast majority of jazz instruction occurs in the educational jazz ensemble, a format that has seen incredible growth in recent decades. "From the early 1970s to the present, the proliferation of jazz ensembles has been unparalleled by any other phenomenon in music education except the growth of concert bands decades earlier" (Mark, 1987, p. 20).

This growth in jazz education can only be viewed as positive; however, the large jazz ensemble format is less than ideal for teaching improvisation. Notwithstanding the many outstanding professional jazz ensembles, smaller jazz combos (usually between three and seven musicians) have typically been both the training ground and the preferred performance medium for master improvisers.

The size and flexibility of such a group provide members the frequent opportunity to improvise at length, to interact, to learn new songs (usually by ear), and to experiment. Because of this, the combo is a near-ideal setting for developing improvisational skills. Through regular jazz-combo experiences, students ingrain a wealth of musical material that forms the subconscious basis for future improvisations. Unfortunately, the small size of jazz combos makes them an unlikely choice for schools. Still, given the tremendous growth in large jazz ensembles, it seems only natural that the qualities of the jazz combo should eagerly be adapted for jazz ensemble rehearsals.

Unfortunately, notwithstanding the increase of educational jazz ensembles, few organizations succeed in helping all students reach their potential as improvisers. Few bands reach the ideal that "everyone in the band must learn to improvise, and is expected to solo when called upon" (Baker, 1989, p. 145).

Some performing groups are jazz ensembles in name only, teaching little of jazz improvisation, style, history, or theory. Some jazz festivals may inadvertently encourage this approach by focusing on the performance of written material while giving little attention to the extent and quality of the improvisations.

Other educators have also questioned the results of a typical jazz ensemble class. "Are students . . . actually gaining an understanding of the music they perform? Are they developing concepts of style and form? Or are they, in fact, only reading notes mechanically?" (Kuzmich & Bash, 1984, p. 14).

AURAL LEARNING

Despite many advances, jazz pedagogy in the school setting still bears little resemblance to either conventions of professional jazz performance or research-based recommendations. Though many educators teach primarily (or solely) through written materials, jazz has traditionally been learned aurally. "The jazz tradition generally elevates aural musical knowledge, with its associated powers of apprehension and recall, to the paramount position" (Berliner, 1994, p. 93).

The earliest jazz musicians had only their ears and intellect to guide them in learning the style. Notwithstanding the many jazz musicians who were also gifted pedagogues and even writers, the craft has remained largely an aural one, and necessarily so. The standard notation that is used to convey most jazz instruction does not, perhaps *cannot*, reflect jazz articulation, swing, and stylistic nuances accurately. These things must instead be learned by listening to and emulating jazz musicians.

SWING RHYTHMS

Performing swing rhythms and articulations correctly is a major stumbling block for many students, mostly because of difficulties with innately inaccurate notation. Of particular difficulty is the subdivision of the beat. Though the actual subdivision of swing rhythm is the source of much debate, "these notes of unequal length are best described as quartereighth [*sic*] triplets" (Collier & Collier, 1996, p. 136). Even this is a compromise (Collier and Collier noted significant nuances in how the beat is subdivided in various performances), and jazz composers have rarely tried to notate swing rhythms according to this rule.

Instead, a group of two swing eighth notes is represented as a dotted-eighth note followed by a sixteenth note, or, more commonly, as what appear to be "straight," or equally divided, eighth notes. Because the notation does not contain all of the information necessary for performance, the musician must personally interpret the music in swing style. "No good notation for it exists. Musicians acquire the style by listening to virtuosos and seeking to emulate them, and they develop a discriminating ear for what 'swings' and what does not. . . . They are not consciously aware of its underlying rhythmic principles" (Johnson-Laird, 2002, p. 417).

Understandably, beginning musicians struggle to interpret swing rhythms and subdivisions when relying on notation alone. Teachers can assist students by personally modeling these patterns in addition to playing recorded examples. When students can correctly imitate a pattern, they should be encouraged to create variations of the pattern.

With encouragement, students quickly translate these skills into both their improvisations and their performance of written swing rhythms. As previously suggested, musicians perform the rhythms without being "consciously aware" of the underlying principles. This does not necessarily mean that they are unaware of the principles, but they simply do not need to *consciously* consider them, as they have been previously integrated into long-term memory.

Even when there is a gap between performance and conscious understanding, it is not necessarily harmful. "Remember, any language is most quickly assimilated through listening and imitation . . . after all, none of us learned to speak by reading first!" (Berg, 2002, p. 43).

LEARNING MELODIES BY EAR

An ideal way to begin assimilating jazz rhythm and style is to learn jazz melodies by ear. In doing so, students begin memorizing repertoire, an essential but often overlooked part of jazz performance. Jazz performers are expected to know a large repertoire of standard melodies and forms from memory. As students learn songs by ear, they are assimilating standard jazz repertoire, songs that are known simply as "standards." They also learn much more, because standards embody the essential "melodic, harmonic, and rhythmic conventions" of jazz style (Crawford & Magee, 1992, p. v). Unfortunately, the failure to teach standard jazz songs and progressions is a significant shortcoming of many jazz programs.

Even a single melody learned aurally helps students develop a sense of tonality and harmonic movement. An additional benefit of learning standards is that many of them have lyrics that students can learn to strengthen their sense of phrasing and pitch. "Tunes to be performed on instruments should include lyrics, which facilitate singing and expressiveness. . . . Unfortunately, most training materials for instrumentalists do not include lyrics" (Schleuter, 1997, p. 47). The existence of many jazz standards that include lyrics gives thoughtful directors yet another avenue for meaningful teaching.

When students memorize the melody to a standard tune, they also ingrain a melodic guide to a standard harmonic form (many jazz standards share identical forms). The task of improvisation is far less daunting for the student who recognizes form (Dust, 2003). With an added awareness of form, students can play the melody with rhythmic variations and then with simple melodic ornaments. These are excellent first steps into improvisation.

Students who are adept at imitating and varying have already begun the important improvisational exercise of interpreting preexisting melodies.

The written melody of a jazz song is seldom performed the same way twice, even by the same musician (Tirro, 1974). Students who play variations on standard jazz melodies are improvising creatively while greatly reducing the difficulty of inventing new material. They also are guided through the correct harmonic structure of the song by keeping their place within the melody.

Learning to interpret melodies also connects students with traditional methods of performing jazz, which may be neglected when completely composed, or "through-arranged," charts are emphasized. "In most school jazz ensembles, passages for improvised solos appear in otherwise through-arranged charts. However, this is not how jazz soloing originated; it began with the earliest jazz musicians improvising embellishments and variations of the melodies of popular songs. Excluding this element in school jazz groups means omitting a crucial steppingstone in learning to solo; it is no wonder that so many students find improvising scary and confusing" (Hynes, 2000, p. 46).

Whether from recordings, radio, or live performances, jazz musicians, particularly improvisers, must assimilate the style by ear. Making jazz standards a part of the material that is learned by ear forms a repertoire of useful and compelling improvisational material. "Developing a large repertoire by ear is extremely helpful for individuals trying to improvise their own melodies, rhythms, and harmonies. This repertoire is important because it helps students develop an understanding of melodic line and a sense of harmonic progression" (Azzara, 1999, p. 22).

RESEARCH ON AURAL LEARNING

Research confirms the benefits of the traditional, aural method of learning improvisation. In a study of the effectiveness of aural versus notated exercises, two groups of novice jazz improvisers received identical material. One group learned the material aurally, and the other group through notated examples. The results "indicated that the aural group produced significantly higher scores that the notation group . . . the experimental procedures produced greater improvement for students who received the aural pedagogy" (Laughlin, 2001, p. 60).

Importantly, students with the least experience posted the highest gains in ability with aural methods, and the lowest with notational methods. This indicates that aural teaching methods are particularly effective for less experienced learners.

Strangely, the opposite approach is common. A survey of experienced jazz educators revealed the following generalization: "The participants incorporate written music when teaching beginning improvisers and less so when teaching advanced improvisers. Most of the participants use written music as a type of crutch for beginning improvisers. As the students become more comfortable with improvising, they slowly remove the aid" (Bitz, 1998, p. 42).

This research also indicated that modeling is most effective when performed directly by the teacher ("musical modeling"), via voice or instrument, and less effective when modeled by a recorded source ("aural modeling"). Again, this is at odds with what is actually happening in most classrooms. "Concerning modeling, the participants indicate that they employ aural modeling more than musical modeling. In other words, they use recordings more than their own playing or singing in class" (p. 47).

APPLYING AURAL LEARNING

Aural teaching methods, such as call-and-response, are more meaningful to students when they can be immediately applied to a performance format. For example, when students aurally learn Mixolydian scale patterns and then reinforce them by improvising in the context of an ensemble chart, the improvisational materials are more fully reviewed and completely learned. As students are given the opportunity to review and revise material over time, it becomes part of their subconscious improvisation repertoire.

The improvisation sections of jazz ensemble charts potentially provide an ideal format for instructors to teach material aurally through call-and-response exercises. Allowing sufficient time and progressing sequentially enables students to ingrain core material into long-term, generative memory. Students memorize melodies, melodic scale patterns (riffs, licks, etc.) in the context of specific (and, ideally, standard) harmonic progressions.

All students need regular opportunities to practice improvising, to mentally evaluate and then perform material from the increasingly unconscious, evaluative stage. Using the same musical materials in direct improvisation instruction *and* an ensemble chart studied concurrently promotes quicker mastery, improved motivation, and greater retention.

APPROPRIATE ENSEMBLE MUSIC

Appropriate ensemble music plays a key role in jazz education. "Selecting appropriate music for the band is one of the most essential areas of concern in the jazz band program. The music is 'where it's at': the essence of the jazz program is based on the music itself" (Kuzmich & Bash, 1984, p. 104). The reason jazz education has grown despite the lack of a formal curriculum is that, functionally, the charts *are* the curriculum.

Too often, jazz educators cannot ascertain the improvisation challenges of new music until they actually acquire it. Such specific information is simply not provided by publishers.

If educators cannot determine the improvisational demands of jazz ensemble charts, they can hardly plan effective improvisation practice using those charts. An elementary school music researcher gave advice that is equally cogent for jazz educators:

> The song materials to be used . . . must be extremely carefully chosen. The song or songs through which the concept or skill is made conscious knowledge to the children must not contain anything new other than the specific new element (tonal or rhythmic) being taught. It is most important that the child find only one unknown in the entire example. Only through this technique can the teacher focus the child's attention on the new learning. (Choksy, 1999, p. 173)

The unfortunate reality is that the jazz ensemble literature in use *almost always* presents students with more than one unknown improvisational element. Perhaps this accounts for the common complaint at high school jazz festivals: that only a few students per band improvise, and that only a few of these correctly address the chord changes (Campbell, 2000).

Efforts to develop sequential improvisation instruction indicate significant advantages to this approach. Limiting the harmonic demands and sequencing instruction from simple to complex enables students to post significant gains in improvisational ability (Coy, 1989).

Integrating improvisation formats with ensemble charts provides additional opportunities to reinforce aural awareness. "Learning is easier when the content is put to immediate use. Success in learning facilitates further success. . . . Frequent review is probably more efficient than drills for reinforcing new concepts and skills. Building on previously learned musical skills is enhanced by review activities that keep earlier learning current and usable" (Schleuter, 1997, p. 29).

Efficient instruction builds on previously experienced musical sounds. By knowing the key of various charts before they purchase them, directors can expose students to a variety of tonal centers, an important aspect of teaching a sense of tonality. "Singing and playing songs in several different modes increases [sic] tonal vocabularies and aids a sense of tonality. . . . The primary goal is to teach the sequence of tonal content and audiation through song literature, not just to teach a collection of songs" (Schleuter, 1997, pp. 69, 72–73).

Jazz educators must find ways to effectively promote improvisation instruction in the ensemble setting. "Good teaching demands finding materials that fit the content objectives" (Schleuter, 1997, p. 151). Unfortunately, although great educational charts exist, they are difficult to identify among a sea of available titles. Without the integration of improvisation instruction with the rehearsal of charts, the prevalent emphasis on concert preparation is likely to trump opportunities for individual expression.

Bear in mind that certain types of charts deserve special consideration. "Standard jazz repertoire with an emphasis on swing style should be the main emphasis. Historically important literature should be performed. . . . Improvisation is central to jazz" (Fleming, 1994, p. 1).

The content of published charts directly affects the curriculum of virtually every academic jazz ensemble program. Fleming (1994) specifically advocates concurrently studying charts and improvisation materials with the same harmonic form (pp. 42–43) and gives the practical advice that "since you probably do not have an unlimited amount of money to spend, it is important to select jazz band music carefully" (p. 19).

"The key to success for any ensemble organization is a knowledgeable director and good literature. Good literature is available, but the director must be able to recognize and select suitable material for his ensemble" (Hall, 1975, p. 80). At present, this level of foresight is challenging, since the improvisational content of charts cannot be readily determined from the publishers' advertisements, and jazz ensemble literature tends to quickly go out of print.

"If outstanding jazz ensemble music is treated as valuable, enduring repertoire, rather than a disposable, volatile commodity, the need for commentary that helps the ensemble director appreciate, learn, and transmit this music is evident. While commentary on jazz ensemble performance practice is available to the director, commentary on specific literature is scarce" (Caniato, 2005, p. 59).

Bear in mind also that the limited information publishers provide "can sometimes be misleading, since their primary function is to sell arrangements" (Baker, 1989, p. 179). Another challenge for directors is that "with more than 300 publishers of jazz ensemble charts, it is not an easy matter to select music" (Kuzmich & Bash, 1984, p. 44).

Despite the fact that learning standard jazz songs is an essential building block of learning the style, publishers frequently avoid standard jazz compositions, partially to avoid copyright problems or additional royalty payments. To be fair, publishers are really just responding to "the majority of jazz ensemble directors [who] program only the newest charts. This forces publishers to release more jazz titles per year since they go permanently out of print much faster than other publications" (Jarvis, 2000, pp. 58, 60).

PROBLEMS WITH CURRENTLY AVAILABLE MATERIALS

A hidden challenge in teaching improvisation is the easy availability of written improvisation materials. Although most of these resources are well constructed, their exclusive use threatens to distance students from the more effective aural approach.

Ellen Rowe said, "One of my concerns is the preponderance of books, videos and other media that spoon feed information, encouraging students to avoid the necessary, time consuming job of absorbing sound and vocabulary. They should learn the music with the same kind of painstaking, organic approach that all the great innovators and masters of the music followed. Students benefit from learning about process, learning how to teach themselves" (as quoted in Garcia, 2002, p. 8).

Another leader in jazz education also lamented the "disturbing trend" of musicians rooted in performing from written sources and attributed it in part to "a change in the way we are taught and learn, in particular a shift from rote to reading" (Baker, 2003, p. 4). This change not only deviates from traditional learning methods but also shows a disparity between research and common educational practice. "The implications . . . to high school jazz programs that teach beginning jazz improvisers infer that published methods of pedagogy might not represent the most effective tradition of pedagogy" (Laughlin, 2001, p. 61).

One obvious example of the difficulties presented by recent publishing trends is the many charts that contain no opportunity for improvisation. Noting that this is particularly true of music for young bands, David Baker observed, "It is my judgment that, with rare exceptions, there can be no excuse for the lack of improvisation space or for the reading of 'jazz solos' at any level" (1989, p. 180). His comment about reading "jazz solos" refers to the now ubiquitous practice of providing a written solo in place of, or in tandem with, improvisation opportunities. Although sometimes touted as an aid for teaching improvisation, this practice tends to reinforce dependence on written music and greatly reduces the likelihood that students will attempt improvisation.

Another significant challenge is that many jazz ensemble charts contain improvisation sections that require students to use unfamiliar or unreasonably advanced material. Instead of being held hostage to the improvisational demands of the charts, educators should choose only those charts that correlate with the sequential improvisation materials their students are learning aurally. "Tasks must be of appropriate difficulty to avoid undue frustration or loss of interest. This is particularly important when teaching music to young instrumentalists" (Schleuter, 1997, p. 29).

CONCLUSION

Although the teaching of improvisation is an integral part of secondary school jazz ensembles, the resources currently available do not promote a sequential method of instruction. Jazz ensemble charts have the potential to be powerful improvisational resources; however, music publishers grade and advertise their music primarily according to the difficulty of the written material within a chart, without any substantive reference to the improvisational requirements of the chart.

Because recordings of charts are sometimes available as a reference, we might assume that improvisational content could be determined through careful listening. Unfortunately, "often recording and score information does not match. The score might have been retouched or modified for publication, changes might have occurred during the recording session, or only a recording subsequent to the original might be available" (Caniato, 2005, p. 62). Consequently, educators are unable to identify the improvisational content of jazz ensemble charts and seldom teach literature that reinforces a sequential improvisation curriculum.

Many educators employ play-along improvisation method books, such as those published by Jamey Aebersold. The large number of these products now on the market attests to their effectiveness, but they are primarily designed for individual, not ensemble, use. In 2003, eight jazz ensemble charts were published that correspond with specific Aebersold play-along songs. This collection of charts enables directors to purchase both the ensemble chart and play-along recording, thus enabling an integration of ensemble and improvisational instruction and practice.

Full-class jazz ensemble methods, such as *Essential Elements for Jazz Ensemble* and *Standard of Excellence Jazz Ensemble Method* also include a certain number of jazz ensemble charts to correspond with their improvisation instruction. Resources from the Associated Board of the Royal School of Music have similar possibilities. (See Chapter 11 for details of books mentioned here.)

Several jazz ensemble teachers' guides contain lists of literature, including *Jazz Pedagogy: The Jazz Educator's Handbook and Resource Guide*, by J. Richard Dunscomb and Dr. Willie L. Hill Jr. (2002). The authors of this book include recommended jazz ensemble charts at differing difficulty levels but offer no indication of the improvisational content. A contrasting resource is the *IAJE-MTNA Jazz Studies Guide* (IAJE-MTNA Alliance Committee, 2001). It includes specific suggestions for the introduction and mastery of improvisational materials and provides an extensive list of songs that reinforce common harmonic progressions. This resource does not, however, list any *ensemble* charts.

Part III of this book includes a list of jazz standards arranged as charts for the jazz ensemble. They are graded and organized according to a suggested sequence for teaching improvisation. Complete lead sheets for each song show the specific chord changes of improvisation sections. While this list is miniscule compared to the complete body of available charts, it provides enough options to help directors choose jazz ensemble charts that match the improvisational abilities of their students, with the added bonus of gaining familiarity with standard melodies and forms. With this resource, educators can readily plan and implement a developmentally appropriate sequence of improvisational instruction that integrates the most common form of jazz education curriculum—the jazz ensemble chart.

5

IMPROVISATIONAL VERSUS WRITTEN DIFFICULTY

One of the major roadblocks to teaching improvisation in schools is that, unlike books and other materials specifically designed to teach improvisation, the various jazz ensemble charts contain wildly disparate improvisational elements. The resulting near-random introduction of improvisational materials in the charts undermines any sequential instruction jazz band directors may concurrently be offering. This is at least part of the reason that so many students struggle with improvisation. The problem is not new.

In a 1978 open letter to publishers of jazz ensemble music, Cliff Colnot lamented, "Though the pedagogy of jazz improvisation is beginning to catch up with the rest of the big band machine, a tremendous gap still remains. Many students can play outrageously difficult passages when they are notated, but still have trouble improvising on a simple twelve bar blues" (p. 88).

Tremendous strides in jazz improvisation pedagogy notwithstanding, this central problem with published jazz charts remains. Even though some publishers have their own in-house guidelines for improvisational content at each grade level, no consistency exists between publishers, and few make their guidelines public. In addition, jazz ensemble charts are advertised according to the difficulty of the written material, without any substantive reference to the improvisational requirements. Consequently, although they may be simultaneously teaching an effective improvisation curriculum, educators seldom teach literature that reinforces developmentally appropriate improvisational skills.

Appropriate jazz ensemble charts certainly exist, but this is of little comfort to the band director who cannot find them. Ideally, charts would be categorized and advertised, not only by the difficulty of their written content, but also by overall improvisational difficulty and specific improvisational content.

Beyond the significant challenge that the improvisational content of jazz ensemble charts is generally unknown prior to purchase, the more daunting hurdle is that many charts require a level of improvisational prowess that far exceeds the publisher's suggested difficulty level. Given that the typical student has had much more experience playing written music than improvising, this approach is backward.

But then again, what is improvisational difficulty? How can something really be difficult when you can personally choose what you play?

While it is technically true that an improviser could choose to play anything, so too could the performer in concert band. But would any concert band director hesitate to correct the playing of wrong notes in a march for fear of stifling creativity? Certainly not. In the classical setting, it is obvious that playing the correct notes is an absolute prerequisite to musicality. Jazz band is no different. Just as the concert band musician has an obligation to *accurately* render the written pitches and rhythms, the jazz improviser must meet the standards of the art form, including choosing notes that reference the underlying harmonies of the song.

And while improvisation is defined by the musician's personal choices, some aspects of performance are beyond the improviser's control. This is particularly true when improvisation occurs in the context of jazz ensemble charts.

DETERMINING IMPROVISATIONAL DIFFICULTY

Following are some of the predetermined factors that influence the improvisational difficulty of jazz ensemble charts.

Tempo

Although the improviser chooses the notes to play and the rhythms to use, the tempo of a song affects the improviser's ability to keep place within the form, to articulate correctly, and to clearly hear the changing harmonies.

Rate of Harmonic Change

The rate of harmonic change is the speed at which one chord gives way to another. As a general rule, the difficulty of a song increases along with the rate of harmonic change, and the rate of harmonic change increases with the tempo. There are exceptions. If individual harmonies are sustained for an extended amount of time, a song with a fast tempo can have a relatively slow rate of harmonic change. Conversely, a song with a slow tempo may change chords as often as every beat, thus producing a fast rate of harmonic change.

Type of Harmony

In one sense, the various harmonies used in jazz could be considered more or less equal in terms of requisite technical facility; however, since musicians typically learn to hear and play music according to a tonal sequence, all harmonies cannot be considered equal in difficulty. A young musician's ability to hear and integrate the sounds present within a comparatively consonant and familiar harmony exceeds the same musician's ability to operate within an unfamiliar or dissonant harmony.

Variety of Chord Types

Progressions that use a variety of chord types are more challenging for students to improvise with and aurally comprehend, particularly when one or more of the chord types is new to the student.

Key Center of Chords

Just as a concert band song in the key of B major would be an unacceptable challenge for most beginning band students, improvisation sections that include chords with less-common tonics add to the challenge of improvising. Ultimately students should attain competency in all keys.

Time Signature

If you thought sight-reading in 9/8 was difficult, try improvising! In truth, the vast majority of jazz standards are in common time. This is partly because shifting the time signature so wholly disrupts the improviser's ability to reference those prelearned patterns, that almost a whole new set of materials (or way of interpreting materials) has to be developed for each new time signature. Consequently, nearly all jazz compositions are in 4/4, cut time, or occasionally 3/4. Most jazz songs with less common meters tend to move back to 4/4 for the improvisational sections.

Style

The style or genre of a song affects many components of the improvised section, including the articulation, harmonies, and subdivision of the beat. Depending partly on personal background and musical experience, certain students may be more naturally adept at improvising within particular styles.

Form and Length

Songs that use standard forms give students the advantage of utilizing transferable knowledge. The length and complexity of the improvisation section affects the amount of harmonic material students must use, as well as the challenge of creating interest and contour over a longer solo. Solo sections in which the form is clearly evident are more manageable than solo sections in which the form is obscured.

Accompaniment

The type and quality of accompaniment directly determines the soloist's ability to hear the chord changes and pulse of the tune.

Visual/Notational Challenges

In terms of jazz notation, what you see is not what you get. The way in which jazz harmony is notated varies widely. Depending on a student's familiarity with the particular symbols used, the notation may clarify or obscure meaning. (For more detailed information regarding interpreting chord symbols, see Chapter 6.)

EXAMPLES

Examples from several prolific jazz arrangers illustrate how these and other factors, when out of balance with written difficulty, can present unwieldy improvisational challenges in otherwise attainable charts. The viewpoint taken here is purposely narrow; we are concerned only with the chart's adaptability for teaching improvisation (a task that it may not have been specifically designed for).

Improvisers sometimes discard standard scale choices in favor of less common scales to address a given chord type. For young improvisers just learning basic materials, this practice can be very confusing. Michael Sweeney, in his arrangement of "Malaguena," notates both a D7 chord symbol and a corresponding scale in each solo part. The scale, however, includes a lowered sixth scale degree and does not correspond to a D7 chord. Regardless of whether the dissonance was intentional, it presents a false impression of what pitches should be present in a D7 chord. Students may enjoy their experience with "Malaguena," but would likely walk away with an erroneous impression of how a D7 should sound and be played.

Some charts contain confusing oversimplifications, such as in "Yardbird Suite," also by Sweeney. In this chart, a G7 chord lasting four measures is indicated. Contrary to the symbol, the underlying harmonies and written solo change chords six times during these measures. Students improvising according to the chord symbol have difficulty reconciling the disparity between the pitches indicated as consonant and the dissonant results they create.

Often the chord changes written for the soloist are more a reflection of the piano part than they are a guide for improvisation. For example,

Mark Taylor's Latin version of "My Romance" contains an optional written solo with chord changes. Strangely, when the written solo rests, the chord changes no longer appear on the solo part. Because of this, the improviser is presented with sudden and random information gaps, making improvisation impractical, if not impossible.

In this and other examples, it seems the written chord symbols are not actually intended as a guide for improvisation. They appear instead to be merely explanatory of the written solo, or a reflection of the ensemble or piano voicings. Many examples of the latter are found when the solo part contains a slash chord indicating both the chord and the bass note. Although this could indicate a polytonal opportunity for the soloist, in educational charts it more often indicates only the bass note of the accompanying instrument(s). Without guidance, this superfluous information confuses young improvisers.

This is also true of extensions such as C11 or C13. The large numbers may appear intimidating to novices but typically do not provide any more significant information than the basic symbol C7. It seems that many arrangers base the notation of their chord progressions solely on part writing and ensemble sounds, without regard for the person playing the melody—the improvised solo that the band is but accompanying. This is certainly contrary to Caniato's counsel that "the arranger [should] be aware of the performance implications of the music they . . . create" (2005, p. 60).

In other charts, such as John Berry's arrangement of "Kansas City," the given solo section may obscure the form of the tune. In this chart the soloist improvises over measures five through eleven of the twelve-measure blues form. The solo works well with the written arrangement, but the soloist is unlikely to gain an enhanced understanding of blues form. Charts like these do provide some improvisation opportunities, but they mostly illustrate lost opportunities for helping students practice improvisation in a more meaningful way.

Many arrangements of standards contain unexpectedly difficult improvised sections due to harmonic alterations of the original tune. "Sonnymoon for Two" in its original version has a basic blues form that would easily correspond to a Grade 2 improvisational difficulty. Steve Owen's arrangement for young band (Grade 1.5 written) complicates this form with the addition of a bridge and a variety of advanced harmonic alterations that catapult the improvisational difficulty of the tune to a Grade 4. These changes sound great in the written solos, but (particularly when the fast tempo is considered) essentially block most soloists at this level from achieving any kind of success with improvisation. Songs like this are ideal for featuring an experienced guest soloist with a young band, but are ill suited for the teaching of basic improvisation.

CONCLUSION

Challenging material is not to be completely avoided; it is essential. However, in order for the material to be appropriately challenging rather than impossibly difficult, directors need to recognize the factors that affect difficulty, and choose charts that help students reinforce current skills while implementing new materials at a workable pace.

Armed with a better knowledge of what challenges are truly present in jazz ensemble charts, directors can choose material that matches the students' ability level in regard to both notated and improvised music.

Part II

TEACHING JAZZ IMPROVISATION

6

SCALES, CHORDS, PROGRESSIONS, AND FORMS

This chapter reviews the basic harmonies present in most jazz ensemble charts, discusses the harmonic functions of chord types, suggests appropriate scale choices for beginning improvisers, and clarifies the various ways of notating these chords.

The information is sufficient to empower an inexperienced educator to identify and teach appropriate scale/chord material for the chords found most regularly in jazz ensemble charts. It is certainly not an exhaustive treatise. (For a detailed discussion of jazz theory, readers should consult one of the excellent references listed in Chapter 11.)

Jazz theory has a reputation for being notoriously complicated, but it need not be inaccessible. Most jazz is functionally tonal and, as in other types of tonal music, jazz chords typically fulfill one of three roles: tonic, predominant, or dominant. Unlike some musical styles, however, jazz chords regularly use extensions and alterations beyond the basic triad. Although these chords usually still function as tonics, predominants, and dominants, their peculiar construction can, at first glance, be disconcerting.

A chord extension is a chord tone outside of the notes of the basic triad (the first, third, and fifth degrees of the scale). Jazz music almost always employs such extensions, an added seventh at the very least, but also the ninth, eleventh, and thirteenth. (The seventh pitch is used so frequently that it is not considered an extension by most jazz musicians.)

While the presence of chord extensions and alterations may cause anxiety for novice improvisers, it is helpful to remember that these additional pitches are simply renamed scale tones. The ninth is the same pitch as a second, an eleventh is identical to a fourth, and a thirteenth is the same as a sixth. Whether indicated by the written chord symbol or not, advanced improvisers and accompanying musicians add ninths, elevenths, and thirteenths to their music at will.

The presence of these additional pitches in the chord is one complication, but the matter is further confused by the variety of chord symbols that may be employed to visually represent each harmony.

The symbols used to communicate jazz harmony to the improviser provide a quick, concise way to relate information. The written chord symbols for an entire solo are commonly called a "lead sheet." Lead sheets typically contain slashes for each beat in place of actual notes, and, above the staff, a chord symbol that relates the harmony being played by the rhythm section. The changing harmonies of a song are often simply called the "changes."

Unfortunately, chord symbols can look daunting to the uninitiated. The symbols currently in use are not standardized and include elements from several systems that evolved simultaneously. Because no standardized system has been adopted, a single harmony may be expressed by any number of different symbols. Composers may use any one of several sets of symbols, or they may mix and match. The inconsistent hodgepodge of letters, numbers, and other characters that must be decoded adds an additional challenge to improvisation.

Improvisers must learn to interpret them all correctly.

Following is a brief explanation of the most common chord types, their typical functions, and their notational synonyms, all expressed as chords built upon the note C. For each entry, the first symbol presented is preferred for teaching improvisation because it is concise and visually distinct from other symbols, making it easier for the improviser to quickly discern the correct meaning.

Bear in mind that chord symbols are just that: symbols designed to express chords, not scales. A variety of scale choices may be possible over any given chord. Additionally, comping (improvising accompaniments in a complimentary style) instrumentalists should remember that although the same scale may be successfully used for different chord symbols, there may be subtle differences in the chords themselves. The following explanation emphasizes only the most common harmonies and the most common scale choices used to improvise over those harmonies.

A GENERAL GUIDE TO JAZZ IMPROVISATION SYMBOLS

Three components of jazz improvisation nomenclature may be present for any given chord symbol:

1. An uppercase letter indicating the pitch that is the tonic of the chord. The symbol C, for example, always indicates some sort of chord with C as the tonic. (Whether or not C is the actual root is another matter, since jazz musicians freely invent their own inversions, or chord voicings.)
2. An indication of the basic chord quality: major, minor, dominant seventh, half-diminished, or diminished. This information may take the form of a number, special character, or abbreviated word.

   - Major chords (Ionian, scale degrees 1, 3, 5, 7)—a letter alone, or a letter followed by maj, ma, M, or $\triangle$.
   - Minor chords (scale degrees 1, ♭3, 5, ♭7)—a letter followed by -, min, mi, or m.
   - Dominant seventh, or Mixolydian, chords (scale degrees 1, 3, 5, ♭7)—a letter followed by 7, 9, 11, or 13. (Occasionally the abbreviation "dom" precedes number.) Regardless of the extension used, it is the seventh note that is lowered.
   - Half-diminished chords (scale degrees 1, ♭3, ♭5, ♭7)—a letter followed by min7(♭5), mi7(♭5), m7(♭5), -7♭5, or $\emptyset$.
   - Fully diminished chords (scale degrees 1, ♭3, ♭5, ♭♭7)—a letter followed by dim or ° and sometimes followed by a 7, as in C°7.

(The difference between the symbols "m" and "M" (indicating minor and major, respectively) can be very difficult to distinguish, especially in the most popular jazz font.)

3. An indication of any alterations or extensions of the basic chord type. Numbers are used to indicate additional pitches that are part of the chord; when these pitches deviate from the normal chord quality, they are preceded by one of the following characters:

   • A minus sign (-) or flat (♭) means to lower the given pitch one-half step.
   • The sharp (♯) or plus (+) signs either indicate a major interval or direct the musician to raise the given pitch one-half step.
   • The plus sign (+) may also indicate an augmented chord.
   • The abbreviation "ALT" suggests the use of the altered scale.

At times, rather than employing symbols, the actual scale to be used is written to the right of the note name, as in C(Aeolian).

The term "add" simply means to add the subsequent pitch to the chord, as in C6add9.

Slash chord notation is a different way of notating harmony. Slash chords, such as C/G, indicate two pieces of information. The first symbol indicates the chord to be played, and the second indicates the bass note. Slash chords can be used to indicate any harmony but are most often used to express a complex sonority as the seemingly simpler juxtaposition of a certain chord over a specific bass note.

At times, this information is pertinent only to chording instruments. At other times the combination of chord and bass note indicates an uncommon harmony or bitonal sound the soloist must address.

COMMON HARMONIES

When analyzing the harmony of a jazz song, keep in mind that mode mixture is extremely common in jazz, and the various major and minor chords are somewhat interchangeable in both major and minor tunes (see Table 6.1).

Table 6.1 Common Harmonies

Chord	Other Notations	Corresponding Scale	Additional Information
C	Cmaj, Cma, CM, C△ Following these symbols, extensions of 7, 9, 11, or 13 may be added. Slash notation: C/C, C/E, C/G, G/C	Major scale	C6 and C6/9 chords use scale degrees 6 and/or 9 in place of scale degree 5, but the major scale is still used for improvisation. These chords typically function as tonics (the I chord). Some improvisers prefer to use a Lydian scale (major scale with a raised fourth). To specifically indicate a Lydian scale, one of the symbols for major chords is followed by +4, #4, or +11. Slash notation: D/C.
C7	C9, C11, C13 "dom" may precede the extension, as in Cdom7. Slash notation: Bb/C	Mixolydian scale (major scale with a lowered seventh degree)	Usually functions as a dominant (the V7 chord) when preceding a major chord. This chord/scale is present in the vast majority of jazz songs, and, like the major chord in traditional harmony, these chords may also serve a predominant or tonic function. Some improvisers prefer to use a Lydian dominant scale (major scale with a lowered seventh and raised fourth). To specifically indicate a Lydian dominant, one of the symbols for dominant chords is followed by +4, #4, or #11.
C-7	*It is important to understand that this chord is not a C chord with a minor seventh, but a C minor chord that also includes a lowered seventh.*	Dorian scale (major scale with a lowered third and seventh degree)	These chords usually function as predominants (the ii chord). Other, less common, possibilities include the following:

(Continued)

Table 6.1 Common Harmonies (Continued)

Chord	Other Notations	Corresponding Scale	Additional Information
	C, Cmin, Cmi, Cm Following these symbols, extensions of 7, 9, 11, or 13 may be added. Slash notation: Eb/C		• minor tonic (use melodic or harmonic minor scales) • vi chord (use an Aeolian scale) • iii chord (use a Phrygian scale) Because the same symbol is used for each of these scale options, the chord's function must be determined by analyzing the context of surrounding chords.
C-($\triangle$7)	A minor symbol • (C-, Cmin, Cmi, or Cm) followed by a major symbol • (#7, $\triangle$, $\triangle$7, Maj, Maj7, M, or M7)	Jazz melodic minor scale (ascending form of melodic minor—a major scale with a lowered third degree)	This chord, a minor triad with a major seventh, functions as a tonic (i) chord in the minor mode. Another form of minor tonic is the C-6. For this version #5 takes the place of 5 in the jazz melodic minor scale.
C7ALT	A letter alone or dominant symbol • (C, C7, C9, C11, C13) followed by • "ALT" or combinations of the following: • #9 • #9 and b9 • #5 and #4 Slash notation: Gb/C	Super Locrian scale also known as the • altered scale, or • diminished whole tone scale. Contains the same pitches as the jazz melodic minor scale one-half step above the given root. For instance, the scale for C7ALT consists of the pitches of Db jazz melodic minor, starting on C: C, Db, Eb, F, Gb, Ab, Bb, C.	Functions as an "altered dominant." (This term refers to chords in which tones are raised or lowered to produce a functional dominant sound within a minor tonality—something that cannot be accomplished without deviating from the pitches of the minor scale.)

				Note also that *anytime* a chord is functioning as a dominant, improvisers may alter it—whether or not the alteration is indicated in the chord symbol. Consequently, this scale may also be successfully performed over other dominant chords.
				The chord extension ♭5♯5 is sometimes used to indicate Super Locrian but (unless used in conjunction with ♭9 or ♯9) more likely indicates an augmented (whole tone) harmony.
C∅7	C half-dim, C∅, or Cmi7(♭5) Slash notation: D♭/C	Locrian scale	Pitches of the major scale one-half step above the root, or the pitches of the D♭ major scale starting on C: C, D♭, E♭, F, G♭, A♭, B♭, C	The half-diminished chord contains a lowered third, fifth, and seventh and commonly functions as a predominant (ii) chord in the minor mode. (In the scale, the second and sixth pitches are lowered as well.) Because the seventh scale degree is lowered only by a half step, rather than a whole step, the chord is not "fully" diminished.
C°	Cdim, Cdim7, C°7 Slash notation: B/C	Diminished scale	The diminished scale used for this chord alternates whole and half steps, with the whole step occurring first: C, D, E♭, F, G♭, A♭, A, B, C. The arpeggio consists entirely of minor thirds: C, E♭, G♭, A(B♭♭).	The diminished chord contains a lowered third and fifth, and a seventh that is lowered a whole step.
				This harmony often functions as a passing chord used to create a chromatic bass line between dominant 7 and/or major chords with bass notes a whole step apart. It may also function as an incomplete dominant chord.
C7♭9	A dominant symbol • (C7, C9, C11, C13) followed by • ♭9	Diminished scale	This form of the diminished scale is formed by alternating half and whole steps, with the half step occurring first: C, D♭, E♭, E, G♭, G, A, B♭, C.	This chord is another common altered dominant used in both minor and major mode progressions.
				C♭9♭13 refers not to the diminished scale but to the following scale derived from F harmonic minor (the pitch a fifth below the given chord's tonic): C, D♭, E, F, G, A♭, B, C.

(Continued)

Table 6.1 Common Harmonies (Continued)

Chord	Other Notations	Corresponding Scale	Additional Information
	and sometimes • +9 • +4 or +11 Slash notation: A/C		Similarly, C♭9 13 refers specifically to the following scale derived from F harmonic major: C, D♭, E, F, G, A, B, C.
Csus	Csus4 Slash notation: G–/C or Gmin/C	Mixolydian scale (The arpeggio emphasizes the fourth degree instead of the third: C, F, G, B♭, D)	This chord is known as a "suspended" chord; the third is omitted in the chord, and replaced by the fourth. Notice that the slash chord notation reveals that these same pitches may also be arranged into G dorian scale.
C7+5	C7+, C+7, C7♯5, Caug7, C7♭5♯5, C7♭5	Augmented scale The scale corresponding to this harmony consists entirely of whole steps: C, D, E, F♯, G♯, A♯, C. The arpeggio consists entirely of major thirds: C, E, G♯ (A♭), C.	Augmented, or whole tone, chords usually function as another form of altered dominant.

Sequences

Although chord types may be learned individually, their real potency comes when understood in context, as part of a harmonic sequence. Rehearsing chord sequences better allows students to hear not only the sounds of the tones, but their function.

The most important sequences are undoubtedly the major and minor mode of the ii-V-I (pronounced "two-five-one") progression. (Although ii-V-I sequences may use many chord types, such as ii^{-7}-V^9-I^{Maj7}, they are abbreviated without extensions in this text in order to simplify reading.) To locate a ii-V-I pattern, first find three sequential chords that progress upward by fourths, such as C, F, B♭. Next, determine the chord qualities. A true ii-V-I sequence consists of predominant, dominant, and tonic chords, and the corresponding symbols for major-tonality progressions are C- to F7 to B♭. The scales for these are Dorian, Mixolydian, and major, respectively. The ii-V portion of the sequence also occurs frequently without a resolution to the I chord.

Minor key ii-V-i progressions are similar, but the chord quality is usually C^{Ø} to F^{ALT} to B♭- (^{Δ}7). A variety of dominant chord types may be used in this progression. Major and minor ii-V-I elements mix regularly in jazz progressions, so that it is not uncommon, for instance, to have altered dominant chords in a major key.

The ii-V-I progression is often preceded by additional circle of fourths harmonic movement, forming a iii-VI-ii-V-I pattern, such as E- to A7 to D- to G7 to C. In this progression, the E- is functioning as a iii chord rather than a ii chord, and the Phrygian mode (the third mode of the major scale, for instance: E, F, G, A, B, C, D, E) should be used.

Be aware that these sequences sometimes progress toward a secondary tonic area in the tune, such as IV or VI.

Form

Harmonic sequences coalesce into a discernable musical form. Notwithstanding exceptions to the rule, most jazz songs use a type of theme and variations format; a basic underlying harmonic pattern repeats over and over, supporting the changing melodic and solo material.

Students should learn to recognize common jazz forms, and should ultimately memorize the chord changes of those forms. Because the same harmonic material is used in many songs, students learning a new song often find that they already know how to play portions of the form. In addition, some standard forms are used for a number of different songs, so that learning to improvise on one tune actually enables students to improvise over many tunes.

An understanding of the overall form of a tune helps improvisers to successfully improvise over any of the smaller portions of the tune. They better recognize the direction of phrases and improve in their ability to keep their place with the changes while improvising. Following are a few of the forms that should be part of every student's jazz education.

Blues   The blues form is the most common and important form in jazz. A basic blues form is a twelve-measure progression that uses a total of only three Mixolydian scales. Multitudes of variations to blues form have developed, including very complex and challenging formats. The blues should be a staple of improvisation instruction at all levels of difficulty.

Modal   Calling modal jazz a form is something of a misnomer. In jazz, the term "modal" typically means that the rate of harmonic change is relatively slow, and that few harmonies are used. This approach to composition can be, and is, applied to other forms. Regardless of technicalities, for improvisers, the fact that the harmonic material changes slowly is a significant aspect of the form.

Song Form   The standard thirty-two-measure song form is AABA, with each phrase usually being eight measures long. The B section, or bridge, typically contrasts with the nearly identical A sections. Although the specific harmonic information in a song form composition varies from one song to another, many chord sequences recur. Other types of song form include ABAB, and ABAC.

Rhythm Changes   "Rhythm changes" refers to the harmony of the song "I Got Rhythm." This thirty-two-measure song-form harmony has been used for a multitude of subsequent songs, so many, in fact, that rhythm changes is the second most common form in jazz.

CONCLUSION

Teaching students to correctly interpret chord symbols, understand the harmonic material they indicate, and organize that material into the larger structures of sequence and form magnifies their efforts exponentially, making each subsequent tune studied more comprehensible, accessible, and enjoyable.

7

SEQUENCE OF INSTRUCTION: AN AURAL HIERARCHY

When teaching rhythm, pitch, notation, or most any other musical concept, following a logical learning sequence is a must. This is especially true of jazz improvisation, where learned materials and concepts must be translated into spontaneously composed melodies. And while the amount of material that jazz improvisers must learn is not impossibly large, it is certainly vast enough that it cannot be mastered all at once. Something simply has to be taught first. A sequence is inevitable, but what sequence is most effective?

With the variety of harmonic choices available, a multitude of viable starting points and ensuing sequences are possible. In truth, any approach that starts simply, moves incrementally, and progresses to include all fundamental materials can be moderately successful, regardless of the particular starting point. The sequence offered in this book is designed to maximize effectiveness by adhering to several guiding principles.

COMPLEXITY

Foremost among these principles is the idea of moving incrementally from materials that are simple toward materials that are complex. Research indicates that, like other subjects, jazz improvisation instruction is more effective when taught with a sequential approach that limits the initial demands upon the students (Coy, 1989). Complexity is, of course, a relative term. When dealing with improvisation, it includes some oft-overlooked considerations:

Aural Complexity

Because jazz, particularly improvisational jazz, has a significant tradition of aural learning, it is particularly fitting that jazz educators should make aural complexity (degree of dissonance) the preeminent consideration in their instructional planning.

Dissonance

Dissonance is an admittedly subjective idea, perceived culturally. Given jazz's nature as a decidedly American style, western perceptions of dissonance apply. Ironically, dissonance is a hugely overlooked factor in jazz pedagogy, an inconsistency that often results in innately dissonant materials being used as an introduction to improvisation.

The prime example of this approach is the exclusive use of the "blues scale" to play over an entire blues progression. (The blues scale contains scale degrees 1, ♭3, 4, ♯4, 5, ♭7, and 8 of the key.) The blues scale is authentic jazz material, used to great effect by masters of the art, and quite easy to learn; however, if used exclusively or incorrectly, it can be hard on the ears. The blues scale obviates important harmony-defining notes (it omits the third scale degree of *all* of the actual harmonies) and creates significant dissonances against the chord tones of each harmony.

These tensions provide powerful ammunition in the arsenal of experienced improvisers, but they can hamper the development of novices. Teaching the blues scale as the exclusive harmonic material for improvisation implies that dissonance and consonance are irrelevant considerations. In the blues scale, students repeatedly play notes that neglect both the sound of the individual sonorities and the tonal gravity that would pull one harmony forward into the next. Prolonged reliance on this approach can make students effectively deaf to the changing harmonies underlying the blues progression. Because the blues scale has no specific corresponding chord symbol, students may even learn to discard chord symbols as unneeded information. Students who have thus become both blind and deaf to the indicators of musical form will produce improvisations marked by haphazard dissonances and little sense of structure.

The teacher who concludes that such an improvisation is "good enough" underestimates both the abilities of the students and the requirements of the jazz art form. Early habits affect students' future abilities to hear correctly and play musically, so it is vital that initial improvisation experiences be more foundational, utilizing materials that are consonant with the musical accompaniment.

Transferability

Another factor to be considered in designing a sequence of instruction is the *transferability* of the material, that is, the level of insight the material provides for future improvisational opportunities. How often will the material be useful in the future? Ideally the most *universal* (and thereby useful) material should be learned first, to give students an advantage in dealing with many subsequent improvisation situations. Material that is most applicable to future formats is most valuable.

Foundational Properties

Closely related to transferability is how *foundational* the material is. Does the intervallic structure of the material provide significant inroads to learning future material? Does learning the material give insights into upcoming activities and experiences?

Connectedness

Lastly is the idea of *connectedness*. Does learning the material prepare the student to play common chord progressions? Does it facilitate connections to larger musical structures, such as standard forms?

Previous Experience

An additional, more pragmatic consideration is the individual student's previous musical experience. For instance, most jazz ensemble students have previously had traditional band-class instruction. Beginning band instruction typically centers on major keys and scales. Building upon these materials not only taps into past learning but also makes use of material that is consonant, transferable, foundational, and has high degrees of universality and connectedness.

Based on these considerations, a rating scale for improvisational difficulty has been developed to categorize and clarify the improvisational content of jazz ensemble charts. It organizes the *difficulty*, not the *quality*, of the material. Consistent with the auditory nature of improvisation, the rating scale emphasizes aural consonance rather than technical complexity. Although the scale is designed to assess difficulty, it also implies a *sequence* of instruction wherein all new material is related to material previously learned and aurally integrated.

GRADING SCALE OF IMPROVISATIONAL DIFFICULTY IN JAZZ ENSEMBLE CHARTS

Grade Zero—No improvisation

Grade 1—Improvised sections contain no more than two total chords and only one chord type.

- Major (Ionian) chords (C)
- Dominant (Mixolydian) chords (C7)
- Minor (Dorian or Aeolian) chords (C-7)
- Moderate tempo, common time

Grade 2—Improvised sections may contain any of the above, as well as the following:

- Changing modalities (major/Mixolydian/Dorian)
- Slow to moderate harmonic movement (rate of chord change)

- Major ii-V progressions
- Major ii-V-I progressions
- Basic blues form
- Standard thirty-two-bar song form—AABA
- Moderate tempo, 3/4 time

Grade 3—Improvised sections may contain any of the above, as well as the following:

- Minor tonic chords (C-$^\Delta$7, C6/9)
- Half-diminished chords (C$^\emptyset$)
- Altered chords (C7^{ALT})
- Minor ii-V-i progressions
- Minor blues form
- Standard thirty-two-bar song form—ABAB, ABAC
- Moderately fast or slow tempo
- Cut time, 6/8

Grade 4—Improvised sections may contain any of the above, as well as the following:

- Diminished chords (C^{o} and C♭9)
- Suspended chords (Csus)
- Augmented chords (C7+5)
- Lydian harmony (C$^\Delta$♯4)
- Lydian dominant harmony (C7♯4)
- Rhythm changes, bebop changes, Bird blues
- Challenging tempo and meter

Grade 5—Improvised sections may contain any of the above, as well as the following:

- Slash chords and bitonality
- All additional chords, including other forms of altered dominants
- "Giant Steps" and other advanced forms
- Extreme tempos and challenging meter

This assessment of improvisational difficulty unavoidably gives preeminence to certain aspects of improvisation while subordinating other worthy considerations. In the grading system, familiarity with improvisational materials receives the greatest consideration. The rating system focuses on developing a sequence of harmonic materials (chords and scales) that leads improvisers both technically and aurally from simple to complex, from familiar to unknown, from consonant to dissonant.

The grading scale includes descriptions of the improvisational materials included at each level. Standard harmonic progressions are sometimes identified in descriptive terms (minor blues, ii-V-I, etc.). At other times, these progressions take the name of a standard song that introduced the chord changes: "Rhythm changes" refers to the harmonic background for the song "I Got Rhythm," "Giant Steps" refers to the John Coltrane song of the same name, and "Bird blues" refers to a type of altered blues form popularized by Charlie "Bird" Parker.

TIPS ON WORKING WITH THE GRADING SCALE

Grade Zero

Grade Zero contains no improvisation. Charts for Grade Zero are included in the index because they can still be correlated with teaching improvisation using standard tunes, for instance with the use of play-along recordings. Directors may also find it necessary to program some charts *without* improvisation in order to leave adequate rehearsal time for extended improvisation study in the other chart(s) to be played.

Grade I

The three chord types learned in Grade 1 are major (Ionian), Mixolydian, or Dorian. Although all three chord/scale types should ultimately be learned, each sonority is to be studied and improvised upon separately in this level, with no mixing of chord qualities in the same song. I recommend presenting no more than two total chords in the improvised material (although the two chords may alternate numerous times). Incidentally, it is advantageous to teach scales in the same way you teach other melodic patterns, through call-and-response. (For a discussion of call-and-response techniques, see Chapter 9.)

At this introductory level it is vital that students learn to hear the notes they play in context with the background harmonies. If the chords change, these changes should not progress quickly.

I suggest teaching major scales first, then Mixolydian, and finally Dorian. Major scales are common in jazz. Although few charts use them exclusively, many improvised solo sections require major harmonies as a part of the improvisation. Major scales are also the harmonic material that beginning jazz students are most familiar with from their concert-band experience. (Many directors wisely make mastery of major scales a prerequisite for joining the jazz ensemble.) Because major chords often serve as tonics, learning this harmony first helps to firmly establish a sense of tonality and awareness of key center.

Once a major scale has been ingrained, students can use that knowledge to quickly learn the Mixolydian scale. This scale may be learned by playing a major scale with the seventh scale degree lowered one half step. Another method of learning Mixolydian scales is to play a major scale beginning on the fifth pitch and ascending the octave. With either method, the new scale is easier to learn if students have previously mastered the major scale. It is also easier to hear, since students need only to recognize a single altered tone, the lowered seventh.

Although they also have other functions, Mixolydian chords serve a dominant function in major keys. By learning the tonic and dominant harmonies first, students have the most important elements of their aural framework firmly in place.

Mixolydian scales are ubiquitous in jazz. Knowing them gives students a strong foothold into a wealth of jazz standards and forms, including blues (the most common harmonic form in jazz). The entire harmony of many blues songs consists of only three Mixolydian chords. Once students have ingrained Mixolydian scales, it is a simple matter to move on to Dorian scales.

When Dorian scales are taught in sequence following Mixolydian scales, only a single new pitch must be learned, a lowered third. Dorian scales can also be learned by playing a major scale with a lowered third and seventh degree, or by playing a major scale beginning on degree two and ascending the octave. Dorian scales are also used in modal songs, songs that use few harmonies and feature a slow harmonic rhythm. A tremendous number of jazz standards use Dorian scales, some exclusively.

Keep formats simple as students assimilate the material from Grade 1; use only charts that have a comfortable tempo and common time. Use of the blues scale is discouraged at this level. Introducing new material too quickly hampers a student's ability to fully assimilate the material. Use patience and rehearse improvisation regularly so that these fundamental materials become deeply ingrained, both technically and aurally.

Grade 2

No new harmonic material is presented in Grade 2. Charts at this level give young improvisers opportunities to practice improvising over more chords and over differing chord qualities within the same song. At this early stage of development, I recommend changing chords at a slow to moderate rate. Already students have access to some of the essential building blocks of jazz: blues form, ii-V-Is, and standard song forms.

Dorian, Mixolydian, and major scales can combine to form an essential chord sequence—the ii-V-I progression. Make a significant thrust of improvisation instruction the mastery of these patterns. In the key of C, an ii-V-I would consist of the following chords: D-, G7, and C. Although the chord tones vary with each chord, the scale pitches are identical throughout the progression. This progression is among the most potent combinations for students to learn: jazz standards are brimming with it.

In fact, an equally valid approach for introducing improvisation is to teach Dorian, Mixolydian, and major scales concurrently, all within the same key (for instance D-, G7, and C). This method emphasizes the overall tonality of the progression and the various functions each harmony plays within it. Because all three scales contain the same pitch material, it is relatively simple to learn them jointly.

As students prepare to move into Grade 3, an extension to the ii-V-I progression can be made by beginning with the minor iii (use Phrygian mode) and dominant VI chords before moving on to the ii-V-I. The resulting iii-VI-ii-V-I sequence is another essential progression for aspiring improvisers.

Grade 3

In Grade 3, students learn the harmonies necessary to perform minor ii-V-i patterns. (All minor ii-V-i patterns are abbreviated in this text without extensions using the lowercase "i" for minor in place of "I" indicating major.) Unlike the major ii-V-I, no single scale or set of pitches corresponds to all three chords of the minor ii-V-i. If undertaken in sequence, however, each of the new chords can be introduced by slightly altering scales students have already learned. While the scales may be technically easy to learn, a great deal of rehearsal with each scale type is needed in order to ingrain them aurally.

As in the major mode, begin with the tonic chord. Minor tonics include the C-△7, and C-6 chords. The preferred scale for minor tonics is commonly referred to as "jazz melodic minor." The pitches of this scale correspond to an ascending melodic minor scale (a major scale with a flattened third). It is important for students to recognize the difference between Dorian minor—which has flattened third and seventh scale degrees and functions as a ii chord—and jazz melodic minor—which has a flattened third scale degree only and functions as a minor tonic.

The half-diminished chord functions as ii in minor keys. Frequently notated as C∅, the triad for this scale is 1, ♭3, ♭5, ♭7. The Locrian scale is recommended for this harmony. It can be learned by playing the major scale one-half step up from the root of the required half-diminished scale. For instance, to learn C∅, play the pitches of the C♯ major scale, starting on C.

Minor dominants are always altered in some way—without alteration, a true, functioning dominant cannot be formed in the minor mode. They are most commonly notated as C7♯9, C7♭9, or C7ALT. These chords are inherently tense, offering ample opportunities for interesting resolutions.

Begin teaching altered dominants through the use of the Super Locrian scale. To learn this scale, play the jazz melodic minor scale one-half step up from the root of the required dominant scale. For instance, for a CALT, play the pitches of the C♯ jazz melodic minor scale, starting on C. While other altered dominant chord and scale options exist, the Super Locrian gives students the quickest access to the defining sounds of these sonorities.

Like the major ii-V-I, the minor ii-V-i sequence is a vital component of jazz harmony, and students gain tremendous inroads into improvisation by mastering both the individual harmonies and the sequence as a whole.

Previous experience with the Dorian scale is helpful in teaching blues scales. Using the Dorian arpeggio (1, ♭3, 5, ♭7), students need only add the two chromatic tones leading to five: 4, and ♯4. With the repetition of the root at the top of the scale, a complete blues scale is formed: 1, ♭3, 4, ♯4, 5, ♭7, 8. While no chord symbol directly relates to the blues scale, the scale may be used to improvise over some minor chords and dominant seven chord types, especially in the context of blues progressions. Use your ears and good judgment to determine when the blues scale is appropriate.

Students who have mastered the materials of both major and minor ii-V-I patterns are already well equipped to improvise over most standard jazz songs. As their mastery of materials grows, they should stretch their abilities by improvising over more adventurous tempos (both faster and slower) and time signatures.

Grade 4

In Grade 4, students learn new harmonic material—including additional forms of altered dominants—and study more challenging forms. Many of these forms, such as Bird blues, use material students already know (minor ii-V-i progressions) to alter forms they are already familiar with (the blues). In addition, new materials are learned in Grade 4.

The Diminished Scale The diminished scale can be used to improvise over two very different types of harmony. It is formed by alternating whole and half steps, resulting in an eight-pitch scale, sometimes called an octotonic scale. (Because of the diminished scale's particular formation, only three configurations are possible, compared to twelve possible configurations for major scales.)

Depending on whether the initial interval used is a whole or half step, the pitches of the diminished scale may be used over C° or C7♭9. If the whole step comes first, the resulting diminished C° contains the following pitches: C, D, E♭, F, G♭, A♭, A, B, C. The diminished chord uses pitches 1, ♭3, ♭5, and ♭♭7 (6).

If, on the other hand, the half step comes first, the resulting scale is a form of altered dominant, C7♭9. The pitches of this scale are C, D♭, D♯,

E, F♯, G, A, B♭, C. Notice that if we spell a D7♭9, the resulting scale—D, E♭, F, G♭, A♭, A, B, C, D—contains the same pitches as C°.

Suspended Chords   Suspended chords use the fourth scale degree in place of the third, but the improviser typically maintains the pitches of the Mixolydian scale.

Augmented Chords   Another altered dominant is the augmented, or whole tone, scale. Commonly notated as C7+5, whole tone scales, as the name implies, are constructed entirely of whole steps. As a result, only two whole tone scale possibilities exist: C, D, E, F♯, G♯, A♯, C and C♯, D♯, F, G, A, B. Notice that this scale contains only six notes, and the arpeggio is made up entirely of major thirds: C, E, G♯ (A♭), C.

Lydian and Lydian Dominant Harmony   The raised fourth scale degree is often used in major and dominant chords. In a major harmony, the resulting Lydian chord may be notated as (C△♯4). When the Lydian dominant is used, it may be indicated as (C7♯4).

Students at this level of development should also be learning more standard forms, memorizing tunes, and improvising over challenging tempos and meters. As the improvisational difficulty increases, so does the likelihood that the harmonic movement employs chromatic, rather than circle-of-fourths, movement.

Grade 5

Materials in Grade 5 have unlimited difficulty. Advanced harmonic substitutions and exotic scales make the material in this level aurally complex. Uncommon harmonies, regardless of complexity, are also relegated to Grade 5. The variety of possible materials, in connection with extreme tempos, adds significant technical challenges.

Although slash chord notation has been used for more benign materials in Grades 1–4, the slash chords in Grade 5 most often suggest complex, even bitonal, sounds. Despite this, rhythm section musicians, particularly piano players, may find it necessary to understand slash chord notation earlier in their development.

CONCLUSION

This sequence for teaching improvisation guides student progress incrementally from materials that are aurally simple and familiar, toward the complex and exotic.

Ample practice time must be given for each new improvisational element. The most efficient way to do this within the context of a rehearsal is to correlate the teaching of improvisation with the rehearsal of specific jazz ensemble charts. Once a successful sequence for improvisation has been determined (even if it differs from the one suggested in this chapter), the director must locate jazz ensemble charts that reinforce this sequence.

8

INTEGRATING IMPROVISATION INSTRUCTION WITH PERFORMANCE CHARTS

Jazz ensembles are, by nature, performing groups. Because of this, it is natural and appropriate that the quality of the group's concert and festival performances should be a prime concern reflected in daily instructional activities. This need not be at the expense of teaching improvisation.

On the contrary, the goal of integrating improvisation instruction with ensemble charts is to teach improvisation in a way that truly improves overall group performance and to rehearse charts in a way that meaningfully improves individual improvisational skills.

Effective improvisation instruction has both direct and indirect benefits for jazz ensemble performance. The most obvious benefit from improved improvisation instruction is that the improvised portions of songs sound better. This would partially eliminate two common complaints at high school jazz festival performances: that only a few students per band improvise and that only a few of these correctly address the chord changes (Campbell, 2000). Improving improvisation is a far superior alternative to eliminating or limiting improvisation for fear of exposing students' lack of skill.

CHOOSING CHARTS BASED ON IMPROVISATIONAL CONTENT

Although other pedagogical tools may be effectively used to teach improvisation, it is essential to connect the teaching of improvisation to actual performance of improvisation. Rather than choosing charts solely based on their written content and then teaching whatever improvisational materials happen to be present, educators must determine in advance the improvisational skills to be learned and then choose charts that facilitate those goals.

By choosing charts that correspond with the improvisational content they teach, educators can improve the performance of the charts while simultaneously teaching improvisation more effectively.

The many advantages to this approach include providing additional opportunities to reinforce aural awareness. "Learning is easier when the content is put to immediate use. . . . Frequent review is probably more efficient than drills for reinforcing new concepts and skills. Building on previously learned musical skills is enhanced by review activities that keep earlier learning current and usable" (Schleuter, 1997, p. 29).

By knowing more about the improvisational content of various charts before purchasing them, directors can plan a sequence of activities. For example, they could plan to teach and review Dorian mode improvisation in several key centers. "The primary goal is to teach the sequence of tonal content and audiation through song literature, not just to teach a collection of songs" (Schleuter, 1997, pp. 72–73).

However, if jazz educators don't know the improvisation challenges of new music they acquire, the probable result is that charts almost always present students with unknown improvisational elements that destroy sequential learning.

In too many cases, the improvisational requirements that confront students exceed their abilities. Difficult charts are neither inferior nor superior; they're simply difficult. It is the ignorance of difficulty that can create damaging inefficiencies.

By obtaining appropriate charts, educators can seamlessly integrate sequential improvisation instruction with ensemble performance opportunities. They can plan a logical sequence of improvisation instruction and reinforce it with performance charts that contain corresponding materials.

In addition, charts may be used to review previous improvisation material, or to introduce new concepts. In established programs, it would be advisable to concurrently rehearse songs that fulfill each of these three functions. For instance, a high school jazz band might choose the following songs for their upcoming concert: a basic blues to review improvising with Mixolydian scales, a song with ii-V-I sequence to reinforce the past term's area of focus, and a song with a single minor tonic to introduce the material to be learned next.

Knowing the specific improvisational content of jazz ensemble charts empowers educators to improve student learning.

For example, teachers instructing students in the initial stages of improvisation can find several charts that exclusively use the same harmonic materials students are learning at the time.

When students have mastered this material, the teacher can choose a chart that introduces a single new harmony exclusively or charts that use a mixture of new and familiar scales. The teacher can avoid charts that would present several unfamiliar harmonies at once. All students in the ensemble actively and simultaneously practice improvisation during rehearsal through call-and-response exercises and other forms of aural learning. Not only do they become more technically adept, but their aural awareness of each successive harmony improves as they are given adequate time to absorb and experiment with each sonority.

In another example, a middle school director who wishes to feature a talented and experienced soloist (perhaps a student who studies improvisation privately) can choose a chart with Grade 2 written difficulty and Grade 4 improvisational difficulty.

Conversely, high school students often enter jazz ensemble with solid music reading skills but little or no improvisation experience. Although they may have three years of music-reading experience, they cannot realistically be expected to improvise at a third-year level; they are in their *first* year of improvisation instruction. To maximize their experience, directors can choose charts with Grade 3 written difficulty and a Grade 1 improvisational difficulty.

In these examples, a disparity between the written and improvised difficulty actually proves beneficial. In fact, matching written and improvisational difficulties is only preferred in the rare situation that students have had equal experience in performing written and improvised music. It's a rare band that has all members improvising as well as they play written music.

Because most charts are designed to include only one or two soloists, a primary task of the director is to provide *every* student with a supplemental lead sheet for the improvised section. Often this means that the director must personally create the lead sheet, but this seldom takes more than a few minutes. (Students can create and even transpose their own lead sheets if the director notates an example.) Practice the improvised sections of the song with all students every day, just like the written sections.

AURAL RESOURCES TO BUILD SKILLS

Two additional aural resources are invaluable for building improvisational skills using jazz ensemble charts. The first is a reference recording of a professional jazz musician playing the melody and improvising over the chord changes of the song students are learning. (Such recordings are easy to find when the band plays jazz standards.) Internet resources now make it a simple matter to purchase a single song, rather than an entire album. If it's not possible to purchase any reference music, search a commercial music Web site for the song. Many provide thirty- to sixty-second streaming audio samples of songs, long enough to hear the entire melody of many standard jazz songs at no cost. Before students ever receive the printed music, consider having them learn the melody of the song by ear.

The second vital resource is a play-along recording so that each student can practice with harmonic accompaniment. This type of resource is available through recordings of professional rhythm sections (like the Jamey Aebersold and Hal Leonard resources), through improvisation software (such as Band-in-a-Box or MiBac Jazz), or from a .midi or .wav file that the director makes personally. Another alternative is to have the band create an original play-along recording. Since the chord changes of jazz ensemble charts rarely correspond perfectly with commercial play-along recordings, having the band make the recording is a great option. Detailed information on devising original bass lines and accompaniments is given in the next chapter.

With the technology available today, band members can easily rehearse, record, and disseminate an audio file of a chart's harmonies in a single rehearsal. (While you should not make copies or distribute recordings of a copyrighted chart, chord changes by themselves cannot be copyrighted, so making your own play-along recording of chord changes for student use doesn't present a conflict. However, be sure to check with your school system or others knowledgeable about copyright matters to see what is permissible. See also the music education copyright center on the MENC: The National Association for Music Education website, www.menc.org/copyright.)

The culmination of improvisation instruction should be an opportunity for students to perform improvised solos, whether in a concert, festival, or just in class. In this way, students can reinforce their improvisation instruction through performance. Consequently, when more students are equipped to improvise, improvisation instruction has an immediate, meaningful application.

The next chapter details specific techniques for maximizing the effectiveness of improvisation rehearsal.

9

INSTRUCTIONAL TECHNIQUES AND ACTIVITIES

In addition to choosing charts wisely, the jazz ensemble director must teach them in a way that maximizes both individual and group success. The techniques in this chapter are designed to help each member of the jazz ensemble assimilate new improvisational materials. These methods are especially potent when used with improvisation materials that are presented sequentially and correlated with the study of jazz ensemble charts.

Only after reviewing the same harmonic material many times do students develop a subconscious reservoir of related improvisational patterns. Improvisation must be rehearsed regularly, and every student must be actively and meaningfully involved.

CALL-AND-RESPONSE TECHNIQUES

The biggest single challenge with improvisation is that it isn't just a single challenge. Improvisation requires using a wide array of skills and knowledge simultaneously. By isolating and practicing the component parts of improvisation, materials become ingrained to the point that students can freely use them to improvise.

Although some aspects of improvisation can be learned through notated exercises, aural learning is more effective and lasting overall. This is partly because aural methods of instruction require students to be active participants. Call-and-response techniques injected with variation are one way to provide meaningful, interesting repetition of improvisational materials.

Call-and-response playing, which also developed in other music genres, has roots in the particular origins of jazz. In spirituals and work songs, the call is a musical phrase sung out by a single person. A response then resounds back from the group, sometimes a literal repetition of the call, and sometimes a variation, or answer to it.

In the jazz ensemble setting, the teacher usually performs the call—a note, rhythm, or short musical phrase. (It is most effective to sing material initially, then to play it.) The ensemble then responds by ear, singing or playing the call back to the teacher. When singing, teachers may choose to use solfège syllables, numbers, jazz articulation syllables, scat syllables, or any other comfortable approach. Using numbers to indicate sung scale degrees has the added advantage of connecting aural experiences to the written chord symbols improvisers must learn to interpret.

Some wonderful call-and-response-based resources and recordings are now available that can be of great use in jazz ensemble. This type of instruction is most effective when delivered "live" by a teacher who can constantly alter and adjust the material based on the immediate needs of the students.

Teachers should listen for the students to correctly perform the melodic fragment (including stylistic details) and then encourage them to vary it slightly, for instance, by maintaining the same pitches while adding variety in dynamics, articulation, or rhythm. In this way, students begin to see the possibilities available to them with even a limited number of pitches and gain confidence in their ability to improvise.

Call-and-response is an ideal method for learning scales, melodic patterns, and rhythmic patterns. As students learn these materials by ear, they also gradually absorb the style, tone quality, and articulation of the caller.

To learn a new jazz scale or arpeggio, for example, the teacher could "call" by simply sustaining the root note vocally. Once all students have matched this pitch, the teacher plays the pitch on an instrument and the students respond, playing the pitch back. It may take several attempts before all students find the correct pitch. Encourage students to keep trying until they find the note. After all, only twelve pitches are available to choose from. If students persist, they can be wrong no more than eleven times. To keep more skilled students interested while the other students search for the correct pitch, the teacher can vary the rhythm or dynamics each time the call is made.

Once all students have found the initial pitch, add a pulse to the exercise, either through a metronome, tapping feet, or a drum-set pattern. Make each subsequent call-and-response fit into a metrical pattern, for instance, a four-beat call followed by the four-beat response. If the material being studied corresponds to a particular scale or chord, consider using an appropriate play-along recording or having the rhythm section comp (improvise accompaniments) to provide the harmonic context of the material.

The next step might be to play patterns using the first two notes of the scale (or chord), and so on, until the full scale has been learned. The particular content of the patterns being played and sung continually changes, even as the ever-recurring harmony becomes deeply ingrained, both aurally and in terms of kinesthetic "finger patterns." For added interest, a more experienced soloist can improvise freely over the pattern while the band is rehearsing the call-and-response patterns.

The primary goal is to build a vocabulary that students can draw from in improvisation. The learned musical materials may manifest themselves verbatim, or in variation; however, when the foundational vocabulary is lacking, the student is ill prepared to build any kind of improvised solo.

It is also important for students to have a solid intellectual understanding of what they are playing. As new improvisational elements are learned aurally, students should be made aware of the corresponding chord symbols, scales, and harmonic functions. This theoretical knowledge is more meaningful if connected with tangible performance activities.

Activities like group call-and-response not only keep all students involved but also help bridge the gap between playing written music in the middle of an ensemble and standing alone to improvise. Regardless of whether we would actually define these activities as improvisation, the momentary event of improvising could not occur without the preparatory process of developing improvisational skills. Through these exercises, students gain both skills and confidence.

As mentioned previously, the jazz combo is an especially effective format for teaching and rehearsing improvisation because each musician is continually improvising in one way or another. By understanding and adopting combo techniques, jazz ensemble directors can greatly enhance the effectiveness of their improvisation instruction.

The most obvious way to do this is to literally divide the large ensemble into smaller combos for a portion of the rehearsal. One challenge to this approach is that most bands have an abundance of horn players but only enough students for a single rhythm section. This need not be a deterrent. Jazz combos exist in almost every possible configuration, including those with partial rhythm sections or no traditional rhythm section at all. The saxophone section alone, for example, can make a very effective combo. With a little searching, recorded examples of jazz masters successfully performing with just about any instrumentation can be found.

While printed music can be found for most combo instrumentations, a better approach is to learn tunes by ear, and to use fake books—music books containing only the melody lines and chord changes of songs—as an additional guide. (With the recent publication of *The Real Easy Book* from Sher Music, even young musicians have access to this format. See Chapter 11 for more information.)

Regardless of ensemble configuration, learning the roles of the various jazz combo members has tremendous improvisational advantages for each member of the jazz ensemble. Aside from the increased ensemble awareness that results from this approach, students become better individual improvisers. And remember, every band becomes a combo the moment the band rests and the soloist begins improvising with the rhythm section background.

Be patient as students learn to improvise, and remember not to confuse practice with performance. It takes time for students to truly ingrain materials. Many initial improvisational activities are formative in nature. They are similar to the strengthening and conditioning activities athletes use to enhance overall fitness. Such drills might never be used in direct athletic competition, but result in dramatically increased ability. Rehearsal techniques that are designed to build improvisational ability for all students simultaneously may become necessarily cacophonous. You'll survive. The resultant improvements in individual and group musicality more than make up for any temporary exuberance. In time, you may be surprised at how good group improvisation can sound.

COMBO ROLES OVERVIEW

When a jazz combo plays standards, they typically perform from memory, putting their own interpretation into music they have played countless times, having usually learned it first by ear. The material is deeply learned, giving the performance a sense of assuredness and freedom. Each member of a jazz combo employs a different kind of improvisational playing to fulfill his or her role within the group. Mimicking these various roles creates a structure that allows all students in the jazz ensemble to simultaneously practice improvisatory playing. This does not mean that everyone wildly solos at once. Far from it. They instead play in a way that maintains ensemble unity while allowing individual choice with selected improvisational elements.

Jazz ensemble directors can help their students attain a similar command of musical materials by teaching scales and patterns aurally through call-and-response exercises. In addition, whenever possible, learn jazz melodies from recordings before distributing written arrangements.

After initial material, like scales and melody, is learned, a solo lead sheet for the chart being studied should be distributed to each student. By involving all students each time improvisation is rehearsed, a common problem in teaching improvisation is avoided: moving on to new challenges before all students have learned the previous material.

Combo Roles: Bass Lines

In a jazz combo, bass players typically improvise their entire part based on the chord changes of the song. Because formulaic bass lines have different range, rhythm, and note choice than other members of the group, these constant improvisations are not overbearing. Teaching students to improvise bass lines is a great way to learn form and scale material, and to solidify their sense of pulse. (Many bass players feel that their most significant role is as a timekeeper.)

Teach students to construct a bass line on a single chord only. Later, when using this technique over an entire solo section, be sure students correctly address each new chord.

Jazz bassists typically play the root of the chord on the downbeat of each measure and chord tones (primarily) on the remaining beats. A good way to introduce bass lines is by playing alternating quarter notes and rests. Through call-and-response, start this pattern on the root of the chord and work for perfect unity in time and articulation (see Figure 9.1). Use of a metronome is recommended.

When a solid pulse has been established, change every other pitch to the fifth note of the scale (the root remains on beat one throughout the exercise; see Figure 9.2). This is similar to early traditional jazz bass lines.

A simple bass line like this should be played in tempo across all of the changing harmonies of any new improvised solo section, using the lead sheets as a guide. With a slight variation in rhythm, pitches one and five also make a decent Latin bass line (Figure 9.3).

While the students play bass lines together, invite individuals to take turns improvising more freely as the soloist.

Figure 9.1   Bass line: Alternating quarter notes and rests

Figure 9.2   Base line: Alternating quarter notes and rests; every other pitch is fifth note of the scale

Once students are proficient at the above examples, construct walking bass lines by eliminating the rests and playing quarter notes on all four beats. While continuing to play the root on the downbeat, invite students to choose any chord tone for beats two, three, and four. (Don't worry about the resulting harmony; since each student stays on chord tones, the overall effect, while atypical, is consonant.)

A basic line might be 1-3-5-3, with quarter notes on each beat (Figure 9.4).

A more typical line that students quickly recognize is a two-measure pattern that integrates a single non-chord tone, 1-3-5-6-7-6-5-3 (Figure 9.5).

Figure 9.3   Bass line: Pitches one and five in a Latin bass line

Figure 9.4   Bass line: Basic 1-3-5-3 with quarter notes on each beat

Figure 9.5   Bass line: Two-measure pattern with single non-chord tone 1-3-5-6-7-6-5-3

Even though the pitch of beat one and the rhythm are predetermined, students are now improvising by using pitches of their own choosing.

Continue to develop skill at improvising bass lines by adding eighth notes on beat four, scale tones on weak beats, and chromatic tones to emphasize chord tones. Study aural and written examples of professional bass lines, and have the band members improvise many patterns over the chord changes of each chart they learn.

What does the rhythm section do while the band repeats the same thing ad nauseum? They certainly don't repeat the same thing. After learning the basic bass lines, they experiment with different voicings and comping rhythms and play the ride pattern on every different part of the drum set. They tremolo, adjust dynamics, take turns resting completely, play busier and sparser, try to imitate their (or your) favorite rhythm section, and in many other ways continually reinvent their improvisatory accompaniments. They can even break into a samba or a ska feel for a chorus.

More experienced piano players can perform the bass lines with their left hand while simultaneously comping or soloing with their right hand. For drummers, time spent rehearsing bass lines is a prime opportunity to practice "feathering" the bass drum on all four beats, or in other words, playing it lightly and in a way that supports but does not overpower the bass. It is also highly recommended that all drummers learn improvisation material on piano, vibes, or another pitched instrument. A working knowledge of harmony and form are of great benefit to any jazz drummer.

The point is that the members of the rhythm section are perhaps more involved than anyone in improvising accompaniments. They learn to feel time together, communicate, and experiment while laying down a solid time and harmony.

Combo Roles: Comping with Pads, Punches, and Riffs

In a combo, piano players (and other chording instruments) improvise harmonic accompaniments in a complimentary style, called comping. As with bass lines, full-band comping exercises involve all students playing the same rhythms, while individually choosing the chord tones to be used.

While this discussion focuses on piano, comping patterns can also be gleaned from other chording instruments. For instance, the pattern associated with guitarist Freddie Green consists of repeated quarter notes, but with a significant rhythmic intensity that is well worth listening to and emulating.

Teach the whole band to comp in the style of a piano player. Three basic rhythmic approaches are easily adapted to the full band: pads, punches, and riffs. Having the whole band play improvisatory comping-style backgrounds while a single soloist improvises melodies is another way that every student in the band can rehearse improvisation simultaneously. This approach also prepares all students to learn jazz piano skills. Whenever possible, take advantage of the visual clarity of the keyboard by demonstrating and having all students participate in theory and techniques on the piano. Eventually you may choose to use these exercises to segue into a discussion about jazz arranging principles, but that's not the primary aim of the exercise.

As with other combo techniques, try to introduce comping aurally, through call-and-response. As students become more adept at mimicking these rhythmic patterns, have *them* take turns "calling out" new material for the band to emulate. With beginners, these techniques work best initially as unison exercises; however, as students gain confidence, encourage them to actively improvise by choosing which chord tone(s) they play. Once the band can successfully perform a comping pattern, have them choose ways to vary it, such as changing the rhythm.

Again, remember to have students take turns playing melodic solos while the band practices improvisational material through the combo techniques.

As these methods are adapted into actual charts, be sure that students adapt to the changing harmonies indicated on their lead sheets. Band members can initially learn to respond with an exact repetition (echo) of the call and then begin varying the response.

Pads   Pad backgrounds are notes or chords sustained behind the melody for an extended duration. Teach students to play pad backgrounds by assigning a rhythm, such as a whole note tied to a dotted-half note, or by allowing students to suggest a rhythm.

With beginning bands, the notes should initially be on the beat; subsequently, syncopated entrances should also be rehearsed. Again students actively vary their choice of chord tones by adhering to the harmonies indicated on the lead sheet. At this point it isn't important that the chord be balanced—the idea is to get them to experiment with correct chord sounds while playing on time.

Initially it may be necessary to write out the chord tones, but also include the chord symbol so students begin to associate the two forms of notation (see Figure 9.6). Eventually, when you feel students are ready, move to using the chord symbol only.

Punches Punches are the short, often staccato chords played behind solo and melody lines. As with the other comping techniques, students should initially play these in unison, then add harmony. While any rhythm may be used for punches, several basic patterns are used frequently. These patterns include the Charleston rhythm (Figure 9.7), Clave rhythm (Figure 9.8), and the "doo-Dot!" (C jam blues rhythm; Figure 9.9).

When singing these rhythms, consider using stylistically correct syllables, such as "Dot!" to express the articulation of separated quarter and

Figure 9.6   Chord tones with chord symbol

Figure 9.7   Charleston rhythm

Figure 9.8   Clave rhythm

Figure 9.9   Doo-Dot! rhythm

eighth notes. Once students have mastered these patterns, vary them, for instance, by beginning them on different beats within the measure.

Another effective pattern is to punch on beats two and four, mimicking the sound of the hi-hat snapping closed. Especially when played with the drummer, this exercise can tighten the time feel of a chart significantly.

Riffs   Riffs are brief, repeated melodic fragments. Students can begin to use riffs by moving up and down scale or arpeggio notes or by alternating chord tones.

An effective way to give riffs some immediate rhythmic interest is to mimic the typical swing ride cymbal pattern while using ascending or descending scale/arpeggio notes (Figure 9.10).

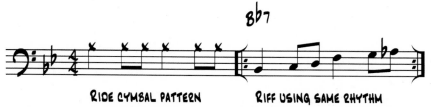

Figure 9.10   Riff mimicking swing ride cymbal pattern using ascending scale notes

Riffs can also be formed by combining pads and punches (Figure 9.11).

Recordings of the jazz greats are another rich source of riffs or short melodic fragments for students to mimic. Whether the fragments are taken from melodies or improvised solos, students automatically glean stylistic and melodic/harmonic insights. The importance of this exercise cannot be overemphasized. Although transcribing an entire solo may be saved for experienced students, with minimal direction, even a beginning student can transcribe the melody to "C Jam Blues," an authentic jazz standard consisting of a two-note melody over a blues form.

As students become more comfortable with pads, punches, and riffs, combine these elements into more interesting patterns. Challenge students to invent their own patterns and then teach them to their classmates through call-and-response.

Combo Roles: Rhythm

The roles of the drum set cannot be easily mimicked by the other instruments. The combo drummer sets the groove, responds to the soloist, drives dynamics, and helps outline the form. Although young musicians often think of the drummer as a timekeeper, a solid sense of time is the responsibility of every member of the band.

It is possible, however, to adapt a particular drum set rhythm or pattern into an improvisation exercise for the band. Take, for instance, a basic swing pattern. We have already mentioned that the bass drum plays a pattern rhythmically similar to the bass player, that the closing hi-hat is analogous to punch-style comping, and that the typical ride cymbal

Figure 9.11   Riff based on Charleston rhythm

patterns for swing can provide foundational rhythmic material for other band members. Invent your own similar exercises by lifting drum rhythms from Latin, rock, or shuffle drum set patterns.

Combo Roles: Melody

When the melody of a jazz song is performed by a combo, it is played or sung in an improvisatory style, with variations added. A great way to introduce any jazz ensemble chart is for students to learn the melody by ear (through call-and-response or from a recording) before receiving the written music. Without this exercise, some members of the band might never play a melody. It is not essential for students to play the melody exactly as it appears in the chart, in fact if would be advantageous for them to hear several different versions in order to hear how jazz improvisers personalize a melody.

Once the melody is learned, have students add their own embellishments, and variations to it. By learning and varying the melody by ear, students attain a melodic guide to the harmonic form of the tune. They better keep their place while improvising, and play their written harmonies and backgrounds in a more musical, cohesive way.

Combo Roles: Summary

At each step of teaching comping and backgrounds, invite soloists to the front of the band to improvise freely (in adherence to the same harmonies the band is playing). This allows soloists more time to practice improvisation while the band is simultaneously engaged in exciting, meaningful improvisation practice.

As students become more proficient at these exercises, they should invent their own backgrounds. This can be done before rehearsal or in the thick of things as students take turns improvising solos. For example, each horn section can be in charge of a chorus of backgrounds. A section leader or other musician can play a new riff alone, and then others can join in. As students learn names for common rhythms, they can also call out the name of the rhythm and the pitches to be used before the solo section begins and automatically launch into a background. For instance, when a student calls out "Clave—1, 3, 5, 3, 8!" the background shown in Figure 9.12 is played.

Such patterns are fun, stylistically correct, and musically effective.

This on-the-fly composition is commonplace in small combos and was also done in swing era big bands, especially those from Kansas City. Listen to any live recording of the Count Basie or Duke Ellington bands, and you are likely to hear some of this instantaneous arranging.

ISOLATING IMPROVISATIONAL COMPONENTS

Irrespective of effective curriculum and pedagogy, students often need additional help. As directors notice students struggling with various aspects of improvisation, it is useful to isolate these problems and rehearse them in a focused way, divorced from other concerns. This is especially true when improvising over challenging formats. For most style and improvisation difficulties, the long-term panacea for both students and directors is to listen to and emulate high-quality jazz as much as possible.

Following are a few additional ideas.

Musical Fundamentals

Gently refuse to allow poor fundamental technique to creep into students' improvisations. If students are not cognizant of using the skills they have previously attained, they are likely to take a sloppy approach to new improvisational skills as well.

When nervousness or excitement causes students to neglect proper tone, air support, and other foundational skills, remind them of their previous progress by having them play a single beautiful note without

Figure 9.12   Background based on Clave rhythm

the pressure of improvising. Then challenge them to maintain their very best sound while improvising, playing a few sustained and beautiful notes over selected measures of the form.

Rhythm

A common rut student improvisers fall into is to play the same rhythm incessantly, without variation. While an effective solo may develop from a rhythmic motif, when overdone, repetition becomes monotonous and ineffectual. This thoughtless habit indicates that additional rhythms need to be deeply ingrained through rehearsal. Here are a few ways to get started.

- Introduce rhythmic patterns gleaned from the charts being rehearsed and practice them as call-and-response patterns. Add variety by starting rhythms on different beats or upbeats, or by lengthening or shortening selected notes.
- Have the students
    - learn and rehearse new rhythms by listening to and emulating excellent jazz recordings.
    - play an entire chorus using quarter notes exclusively.
    - play an entire chorus using continuous swing eighth notes exclusively.
    - play an additive chorus: one in which the first phrase is a single note, and each subsequent phrase is one note longer.
    - play a single pitch on each chord while improvising new rhythms.
    - transcribe (notate) rhythms learned through call-and-response.
- Rehearse rhythmic theme and variations patterns. For this exercise, a brief rhythmic pattern is designated as A and is repeated as part of a larger sequence that includes elements of variety in the form of other rhythms designated as B or C. Effective patterns include AAAB, AABA, and ABAC.

Note Choice

Difficulty playing pitches that correspond with the harmony of the song can stem from a number of factors:

- Lack of fluency and aural familiarity with scale material and chord changes
- Getting lost in the form
- Inability to keep pace with the rate of harmonic progression

If students do not grasp the scale material for each of the harmonies in the solo section, review this material through call-and-response activities.

To strengthen a sense of the overall form, have them play the entire form, using only the roots of each chord. Then, in a similar manner, play the other chord tones, then scale tones of each harmony.

If the rate of harmonic progression is too fast, either slow down the entire tempo or limit the student in some way. For instance, confine them to playing the first three notes of the scale exclusively. Or have them rest during certain measures in order to keep their place while still playing appropriate material when they do play.

Solo Development

Despite skill at improvising short phrases, students may not understand how to develop the material they are playing. Two simple approaches are to vary the pitch and the rhythm of the initial musical statement in a way that is based on, but not the same as, the original. Have the student

- use a single rhythm throughout one full chorus of improvisation, changing the pitches on every repetition.
- improvise on a single pitch for an entire chorus, creating interest solely by varying the rhythms used.

Space

A lack of rests in an improvised solo fatigues the listener and performer alike. In the heat of the moment, however, some students never want to pause.

- Conduct the improviser, indicating to them when to pause and when to resume playing.
- Map out a plan for the location and duration of rests within the form, and then have the student play accordingly.

- Reverse soloist roles with a comping instrument, with the former soloist playing only during rests and long notes in the other student's solo.

Interaction

The term "soloist" could easily lead students to misunderstand the interactive role they should be playing while featured as an improviser with the ensemble.

- Trading phrases. Without worrying about which pitches are used, have students practice trading conversational solos with other band members. One student calls, singing or playing a phrase, and another (or others) answers. Start with literal repetition of the material called out, but work into question-and-answer-type interaction. This exercise is particularly useful for the rhythm section, and they can continue it during subsequent improvisation rehearsal, interacting with and commenting musically upon the things performed by the soloist.
- Student-led call-and-response. After hearing a call from a band member, the teacher responds, altering the material slightly.
- Communication models. Have students tell a knock-knock joke and then use musical call-and-response to recreate it via instruments. Try similar exercises with other interactive dialogues.

Melodicism and Phrasing

- Have the students learn the melody of a jazz standard by ear, either from recordings or live call-and-response.
- Using neighbor tones, dynamics, and rhythmic alterations, students should personalize the melody into their own artistic statement.
- When applicable, have students learn the lyrics of the song and sing them to discover phrasing possibilities.
- Have students make phrasing cohesive by emulating speech patterns, especially poetic verse, rhymes, or song lyrics; they should try to play musical lines that have similar phrasing.

Dynamics

It has been said that there are two kinds of beginning improvisers: those who play so quietly you can't hear them, and those who blast so loudly that you wish you couldn't. In fact, a third type exists: those who know how to play with good tone and vary their dynamics. Here are some exercises your students can do:

- Sustain a specific, predetermined note over the entire form. Experiment with changing dynamics while playing with accompaniment.
- Clap on each beat of the solo section, adjusting the loudness as you would while soloing.
- Create dynamics vocally with a play-along recording, contrasting shouts, whispers, and normal speech volume.

Special Effects

The most common problem with special performance effects, such as growling, is that they tend to get far too much emphasis from young improvisers. Ask students to choose a single effect, like a growl, and describe the emotional impact that effect conveys. They should consider how that emotion best fits into the overall contour of the solo and perform it at only one chosen moment during a solo.

Overall Shape

To help students visualize the shape of a section, have them

- draw various intensity maps, or charts, or just discuss the intended ebb and flow of intensity during a solo.
- raise and lower instruments while playing to show awareness of increasing and decreasing intensity while playing or listening to a recording of an improvised solo.
- conduct in a way that demonstrates the desired shape.

Form

Even when students have the knowledge and skills necessary to play the various harmonies in a solo section, they sometimes struggle to keep their place while improvising. This usually results from a lack of awareness of the form, combined with the numerous beat-by-beat challenges that students focus on to the exclusion of form.

An understanding of the form of a chart can greatly enhance students' ability to keep their place while improvising. Unfortunately, not all jazz ensemble charts call for students to improvise over a complete chorus of the form. The following methods, while especially effective in full-form solo sections, can also aid in the rehearsal of whatever portion of the form is used.

A sense of form, like other musical knowledge, can become ingrained and automatic. This only happens after form has been consciously and carefully rehearsed. The following ideas can be applied to both the complete form, and the shorter harmonic sequences within the form.

- Make and distribute lead sheets to each student.
- Ask students to begin learning a new chart by singing, playing, and memorizing the roots of the chord progression.
- Have students improvise rhythmically through the form, using roots only while changing chords on time.
- Teach stylistic exercises, like interpreting long notes with an fp accent and crescendo, while playing roots over the form. (This type of exercise makes a great warm-up for the band.)

Incidentally, the idea that roots are to be avoided while improvising has been vastly overstated, especially when dealing with beginning improvisers. Students need to be aware of the movement of the chords, and playing roots helps them to hear the changes. Besides, while the root may not be the most evocative sound in a chord, it is an important sound. The root may be interpreted as the tone of rest; music needs moments of release as well as tension. Once students have memorized and ingrained the root movement of the chords, repeat these exercises using other chord tones.

Additional ideas for improving awareness of form follow:

- Decrease the tempo.
- Rehearse improvisatory bass lines and comping patterns over the form. (Be sure to change notes according to the shifting chords.)
- Have students learn the melody by ear.
- Ask students to notate guide tones, or important harmonic notes for each chord, on the lead sheet and play the entire form using

only these notes. The third and seventh notes of chords are usually good notes for feeling harmonic progressions because they tend to resolve by half step into the next chord. Have students rehearse the form playing only guide tones.

- Ask students to play a single note over top of the entire form and identify instances when it sounds most and least consonant.
- Color-code the lead sheet for students. Use a different color for every four measures, for the bridge, and so on. Make it visually easy to see the things the improviser is hearing.
- Have the band chant the form vocally, saying chord names in tempo, with a recording, or with a rhythm section accompaniment.
- Play Name That Change. Play a recording of the solo section, but start somewhere unexpected, perhaps in the middle. Ask students to identify the part of the solo section that is heard.
- Have students identify major events. While listening to a recording or the rhythm section, students raise their hands to show awareness of when backgrounds enter, chords change, modulations occur, or new sections begin.
- Assign each student to improvise over a single measure of the form. The music should stay in tempo as each student improvises her solo.
- With a partner or as a call-and-response exercise, have students trade one-, two-, or four-measure solos over the form, using roots only.

When a new song is approached in this way initially, the form becomes deeply ingrained and serves as a driving force for better phrasing, balance, intonation, and note choice.

Despite exceptions to the rule, most jazz ensemble charts use a type of theme-and-variations form that offers additional ways to connect the learning of improvisation with the rehearsal of the chart. The basic harmonic pattern, or form, of most charts repeats over and over as a foundation for everything else that occurs. Initially it may underlie two repetitions of the melody. Then perhaps the form repeats again beneath a solo section. Next, it may support a saxophone soli and then repeat yet again during a shout chorus. Throughout all of this varied musical material, the harmonic pattern has repeated itself basically unchanged.

Because a recurring harmony underlies the entire chart, many written phrases share the same chord structure with each other and with portions of the improvised solo section. When rehearsing a portion of the improvised solo, locate written passages built upon the same harmony. Practice (loop) these written passages as a background while a soloist practices improvising over this portion of the form. In this way, the band perfects and tightens the written material, while the soloist gets extended practice over a smaller portion of the solo.

The written figures, regardless of what instruments may play them in the arrangement, can also be learned aurally by the entire band. An outstanding exercise is to then have the entire band learn a few of these figures in all twelve keys. This turns the passage into an improvisational lick that can be used in future solos.

Entire charts can be practiced this way, one small section at a time. A soloist can even solo over the entire song in rehearsal, following the form over and over again. By relating chord changes to the written sections as well as the improvised section, band members begin to perceive form and harmonic progression throughout the composition, adding greatly to their sense of phrasing and intonation.

Creativity

Creativity is an eventual musical coalescence of everything else; however, it is possible to draw it out deliberately.

Singing is one of the most effective shortcuts for getting the student's inner ideas to emerge during improvisation. Humans are musical by nature, and with no intermediary instrument, sung improvisations tend to automatically align with the harmonic requirements of the form while being melodic. It does not matter at this point what syllables a student sings. Students should simply recreate the sounds they hear in their head. Playing recordings of improvised vocal "scat" singing for the band may help them to overcome timidity and enjoy the experience of improvisational singing.

A fun way to encourage students that are especially hesitant to sing is to give them a kazoo. In terms of teaching improvisation, humming through a kazoo accomplishes the same goals as singing, and is so overtly silly that few students can resist the temptation to try it.

To connect this innate musicality with instrumental skills, have students sing their own phrase (over harmonic accompaniment), then learn to play it on their instrument. Encourage them to sing over the same background chord changes several times, until they are satisfied with the result. For longer solo sections, do the same activity for the whole form. As an added step, have students record and literally transcribe (notate) their own solo. Students are usually surprised to discover how well their improvised singing corresponds with the harmonies of the song.

By transcribing this highly personal improvisation to the instrument, students learn to trust their instincts and to better make the connection between what is happening in their heads with what happens through their instruments.

Another avenue to creativity is to learn (by ear) improvisations and melodies performed by personally admired jazz musicians and then alter it, or apply the style of the performer to a new song. Over time, as these various sounds are ingrained, they combine and evolve into a unique personal approach, one made of many component influences.

Emotional Impact

Practice improvising with the sole purpose of expressing assigned emotions. Ask students to choose a specific word to describe an emotion and try to express that feeling musically. Tell them to be creative and go beyond happy and sad to more evocative emotions like exuberance, jealousy, or sullenness. For a greater challenge, have students try improvising emotion-inducing ideas like conflict, freedom, or equality. Challenge students to come up with their own evocative words, perhaps taking them out of schoolbooks.

Once they are comfortable with improvising according to assigned emotions, challenge students to think of an emotion or situation they have experienced in the last week, and to improvise in a way that might express it. Then have the rest of the band guess what the soloist was trying to relate.

Approach these exercises with good humor, and realize that the initial, proximate goal is simply to connect the students' emotions with their playing; movingly expressive solos come later.

Listen to master improvisers and ask students to react to what emotional impact the music has on them. (Almost any John Coltrane recording is great for this kind of exercise.) This may even help students to understand why some music is intentionally jarring or that music can have a role beyond mere entertainment.

Transcribing

No group rehearsal techniques can benefit individual musicians as much as intense personal practice, especially if a large portion of that effort is directed toward emulating great jazz musicians. Learning to play the improvisations of the masters by ear is an invaluable exercise. Encourage students to do more than simply copy the pitches. They should strive to assimilate the tone, articulation, and style of each performer studied. This kind of activity can be accomplished in small degrees in the ensemble as melodies and improvisational materials are learned through call-and-response.

CONCLUSION

By simplifying, isolating, and rehearsing the various components of improvisation, constant progress is achieved. To some, these exercises may seem predictable and uncreative, but they propel students into new ways of playing and ultimately unlock far greater creativity than an approach that allows students to linger in comfortable and unproductive habits. Challenge students to find unique ways of organizing musical materials within the prescribed limits. This task is actually far easier than responding to vague directions to "make something up."

When teachers are faced with an instructional challenge that seems untenable, they need not despair, but instead can take what they know and thoughtfully improvise a technique of their own.

⑩

SUGGESTED STANDARDS AND
ASSESSMENTS FOR IMPROVISATION

Although many schools now award academic credit for jazz ensemble, few use standards or assess student learning in improvisation.

Difficulty in assessing improvisation is partly due to the fact that improvisation encompasses a wide range of skills. It includes all of the musical concerns found in a more traditional performance medium like a solo festival, with the added complication that the soloist must spontaneously compose the melody.

Some educators avoid assessment for other reasons, fearing that examining improvisation too closely might destroy creativity. Far from it. By presenting clearly structured instruction and assessment activities, jazz educators empower their students to proceed quickly and with confidence.

The very nature of jazz improvisation suggests that making certain elements fixed and unchanging grants the musician even greater freedom with those elements that remain variable. In many ways, structure is a prerequisite for creativity. This is especially true for young students. Imagine giving an instrument to a new student, but refusing to teach him how to assemble it for fear of stifling creativity. It is unlikely that this approach would lead to anything other than frustration for all involved. Similarly, jazz students desperately need guidance in order to "put together" the varied elements of improvisation. Assessment, at its core, is just that—guidance that helps students to learn.

Bear in mind, however, that the traditional methods used to measure achievement in other, less multifaceted subjects may not be the best tools for assessing jazz improvisation. It is doubtful that jazz students will ever demonstrate all they know by filling in bubble sheets, or that jazz educators will be able to accurately quantify aesthetic reactions. On the other hand, jazz improvisation is ridiculously well suited for authentic assessments, wherein students show mastery of learned skills through performance.

But how do we deal with the innate complexity of assessing a creative act? One key to useful, productive assessment is to isolate the component skills and knowledge that lead to improvisational success. By examining each element separately, accurate, meaningful, and measurable improvisation assessments can be made.

Improvisation is only one part of a full music education, so it is natural to assume that all-inclusive music education models, like the National Standards, exceed its scope. This is probably true. After all, some valuable musical experiences and skills simply cannot be accomplished through improvisation alone.

To take another viewpoint, however, it would be very useful to reference clear standards for "what students should know and be able to do" (National Arts Education Association, 1994, p. v) in regards to jazz improvisation. An example of possible standards in jazz improvisation can be derived by liberally adapting the National Standards to address the specialized concerns of jazz improvisation.

Upon close inspection, the resulting standards for jazz improvisation retain a great deal in common with the original National Standards. Perhaps this is because success in improvisation requires total musicianship, the same goal as any music program.

Still, some necessary differences exist. In these adapted standards, playing instruments and singing are not two separate concerns, but are intertwined. Singing is an important link that connects the ability to hear music (literally and mentally) and the ability to play heard music by ear on an instrument. Because this skill is a vital part of jazz improvisation, both vocal and instrumental methods of creating music are essential to developing improvisers.

There is a bias, of course. In jazz ensemble, the emphasis is clearly on instrumental performance, not vocal finesse. In terms of improvisation exercises, if students can sing correct pitches with appropriate style, they have met the standard. Students specifically interested in jazz singing should supplement their instrumental improvisational activities with musical fundamentals designed specifically for vocalists.

The following standards, while not definitive, are one example of how defining *what* is to be learned can clarify *how* it is to be assessed.

CONTENT STANDARD 1:

Performing varied music and musical materials learned by ear

Achievement Standard   In response to aural models, including recordings and call-and-response exercises, students first vocally, and then on instruments, repeat a variety of music and musical materials verbatim. Materials used should correspond with the appropriate level of difficulty and should include

1. single sustained pitches.
2. scales and scale fragments (stepwise motion).
3. scale patterns (including arpeggios and other skips).
4. melodies in a variety of styles, including standard jazz melodies.

In addition, the student demonstrates ability to play from memory the requisite scales related to the chords, chord sequences, and forms of the appropriate difficulty level.

CONTENT STANDARD 2:

Improvising variations and accompaniments within specific guidelines

Achievement Standard   Students improvise, vocally and on instruments, by adhering to specifically limited roles and by creating variations. Materials used should correspond with the appropriate level of difficulty and should include

1. variations on given scales, rhythms, melodic fragments, and related patterns.
2. improvised variations of given melodies.
3. improvisation in the style of a bass line.
4. improvisation in the style of comping patterns.

CONTENT STANDARD 3:

Improvising melodies

Achievement Standard   Materials used in improvisation should correspond with the appropriate level of difficulty and should allow students to demonstrate

1. use of learned patterns.
2. variations of learned patterns.
3. note choices that correspond with underlying harmonies.
4. ability to connect one harmony to another through varying melodic and harmonic approaches.
5. growing mastery of the components of improvisation.[1]

CONTENT STANDARD 4:

Understanding jazz harmony (inroads toward composition and arranging)

Achievement Standard   Using scale and chord material from the appropriate difficulty level, students

1. describe the harmonic functions of various chords.
2. recognize standard harmonic sequences and forms by sight and by ear.

3. write from memory the form of a song, including chord symbols.
4. invent a background to correspond with a given chord sequence by combining learned improvisational patterns, and notate that background.
5. in a combo setting, determine the instrumentation for the melody and improvised sections.
6. analyze a written solo or solo transcription to determine the extent to which chord changes are represented in the improvised melody; account for any notes that do not seem to correspond directly with the harmony.

CONTENT STANDARD 5:

Reading and notating improvisation symbols

Achievement Standard   Using scale and chord material from the appropriate difficulty level, students

1. read chord symbols and interpret them by writing or describing the chord name and corresponding scale.
2. read chord symbols and interpret them by performing the corresponding chord and/or scale from memory.
3. read chord symbols and interpret them by improvising using the corresponding chord and/or scale material.
4. notate chord symbols to correspond with given chords or scales.
5. notate alternate chord symbols for a given chord and explain any nuances in meaning between chord symbols that are similar.

CONTENT STANDARD 6:

Listening to, analyzing, and describing jazz improvisation

Achievement Standard   As often as possible, students listen to a wide variety of recorded jazz and attend live jazz performances. In response, students

1. identify stylistic elements that correspond with particular jazz styles and eras.

2. identify instances where chords change and also where the form repeats.
3. identify the form of the song.
4. sing and/or play along with the music (when possible) and determine by ear the key, harmony, and melodic content.
5. describe a personal, emotional response to an improvised solo that affected them in a noticeable way.

CONTENT STANDARD 7:

Evaluating improvised music

Achievement Standard   Students

1. evaluate the quality of improvised music, including self-evaluation through recordings.
2. evaluate how each of the various components of improvisation affects the quality and character of the music.
3. compare and evaluate improvised performances of the same song by different musicians. If one performance was more enjoyable and emotionally satisfying, determine specific aspects of the performance that contributed to this impression.
4. compare the experiences of listening to jazz recordings and attending live performances.
5. evaluate how improvisation relates to other disciplines.
6. evaluate how the components of jazz improvisation, such as use of space, compare with other creative disciplines, such as musical composition, visual and performing arts, and writing.
7. compare how various emotions might be expressed in both improvisation and other art forms.
8. identify other improvisational genres (historic or contemporary) and evaluate how they compare to jazz improvisation.

CONTENT STANDARD 8:

Interacting and communicating through improvisation

Achievement Standard   In order to interact with other musicians and audience members during improvisation, students

1. use eye contact, facial expressions, and subtle gestures.
2. adjust personal performance in response to the playing of another musician, for instance, by playing complimentary phrases in response to other performers.
3. exhibit confidence and poise, appropriate dress and demeanor.
4. choose musical materials that express personal emotions.
5. respond positively to the performances of other musicians.

CONTENT STANDARD 9:

Understanding improvisation in relation to history and culture

Achievement Standard   Students

1. explain how jazz musicians have reacted to historical events and social conditions, both musically and personally. Give specific examples.
2. evaluate how the improvised solo performance of a historically significant jazz musician may reflect the culture or emotions of their time period.
3. identify other improvisational genres existing today and consider how the differences between these genres and jazz improvisation might reflect differences in the history and culture of the musicians and larger societies.
4. explore the process and practice of improvisation in styles of music other than jazz. Explain similarities and differences.

It is worth noting that while activities like composition are, by definition, excluded from this list of improvisation standards, they should certainly be a part of the total jazz ensemble curriculum and are closely related to improvisation. In fact, composition is a natural outgrowth of improvisation. One exercise that is useful to both endeavors is to invent, notate, and perform melodies and backgrounds fitting a given harmonic form, such as the blues.

ASSESSMENT IDEAS

By using standards such as those previously suggested and by understanding the components of improvisation, such as those listed in Chapter 3, jazz ensemble directors can develop meaningful assessment techniques. An effective assessment is one that accurately measures progress while promoting student learning.

Formative assessment methods suit improvisation particularly well, partly because the music itself is constantly changing. Most music teachers already use formative assessments as a routine part of their rehearsals. For example, when a student plays an incorrect pitch, the director may stop to ensure that the student knows the correct fingering. The student must then demonstrate an ability to play the correct pitch before regular instruction resumes. Few directors consider techniques like this assessment, but by continually monitoring student performance and adjusting instruction to maximize student learning, music teachers give a model of formative assessment that should be the envy of the educational community.

Jazz ensemble directors can continually assess improvisation in a similar way. They should not hesitate, for example, to pause and correct inappropriate notes in an improvised solo. When students are rehearsing improvisation, however, directors do not point out *the* correct pitch, but might instead suggest *several* appropriate pitch choices.

Summative assessments are less commonly made in jazz improvisation. One example of a summative improvisation evaluation is the evaluation made by a jazz festival adjudicator. Adjudicators typically assess the overall effectiveness of the solo, and perhaps comment specifically on a few items. Such assessments can be very useful, but, due to time limitations, are usually cursory and limited to only a few members of the ensemble.

For directors involved in ongoing instruction, a more effective method is to regularly isolate and assess the individual standards and the elements of improvisation. It is not necessary or even desirable, to assess every aspect of improvisation every day. Focus instead on a single standard each day, or each week, until all of them have been addressed. For example, for a specific chart that is being rehearsed, choose a different component of improvisation to focus on each week. Let the students know in advance how they are to be evaluated, and at the end of the week give a focused, meaningful assessment on the material that has been rehearsed that week.

Keep in mind that the improvisational material to be taught and assessed ought to correspond with the students' ability and experience level. Using the Rating Scale for Improvisation Difficulty helps ensure that attainable challenges are offered and appropriate assessments are given; individual adjustments may still be needed. Fortunately, improvisation is a wonderful format for simultaneously involving students of different abilities.

For example, if a challenging format is being introduced, a director may determine that beginning students are making adequate progress toward Improvisational Standard 3.1 (improvise note choices that correspond with underlying harmonies) if they play whole notes over the form that correspond with each chord.

If a less difficult chart is being studied, advanced improvisers can practice new variations of the material or even substitute chords. (As professional jazz musicians continually prove, the musicality and virtuosity than can be displayed over a B♭7 chord is virtually unlimited.)

It is up to the teacher to determine the progressive level of difficulty that best leads students toward fully meeting each standard. Make sure students are informed so that they too can focus their efforts and make discernable progress.

Types of Assessment

Many types of assessments can be used to measure progress and achievement in jazz improvisation.

Participation   Improvising for the first time can be daunting. Students demonstrate great courage when they play alone for their teacher and peers. This kind of courage breeds confidence, a necessary part of improvising and interacting. Let students know that effort counts and applaud it; but don't let it be the only thing that counts.

Focused participation, or group assessment, is a more effective assessment tool. In this type of assessment, the instructor simultaneously evaluates multiple students. A prime example of this is group assessment through call-and-response activities. The director carefully listens as the group responds to the given melody, evaluating their competence. When the entire group plays it correctly, the director knows instantly that they have mastered the material (at least initially).

Focused participation can be adapted to assess other tasks as well. Students listening to a recording can collectively raise their hands when they hear the form repeat. They can say the names of chords out loud from memory while listening to a play-along recording. They could even shout wildly anytime they hear the teacher play an intentional wrong note while modeling the guide tones of a harmonic sequence. In order for these exercises to be effective, the director must be vigilant to ensure that all students participate.

Written Tests and Quizzes Jazz theory knowledge can be readily assessed through traditional pencil-and-paper tests. For instance, fill-in-the-blanks, and multiple-choice questions are fast and direct methods for discovering whether students know scale and chord names. Students can also notate chords, scales, or sample melodic phrases on a lead sheet. Beyond these obvious examples, teachers can devise simple listening forms on which students can map changes in dynamics, intensity, or interaction. Whenever possible, augment such exercises with corresponding performance assessments that examine the student's ability to play the material.

Rubrics Rubrics clearly show student achievement on a continuum of differing levels of competency. Once standards have been established, rubrics are a great way to assess improvisation. They are particularly effective because students and parents can easily understand the student's current level of ability as compared to the standard.

Following are examples of two types of rubrics that may be used to assess jazz improvisation. One uses a number system (with 4 being the highest possible score, and 1 the lowest) and details specific content to be demonstrated:

Standard 5.1: Read chord symbols and interpret them by writing or describing the chord name and corresponding scale.

4—Student reads and interprets all chord symbols in Grade 1. Student demonstrates knowledge of both the chord names and corresponding scales.

3—Student reads and interprets two of the chord symbols in Grade 1. Student demonstrates knowledge of two chord names and corresponding scales.

2—Student reads and interprets one of the chord symbols in Grade 1. Student demonstrates knowledge of one chord name and corresponding scale.

1—Student does not read or interpret the chord symbols in Grade 1.

The other type of rubric is more subjective, allowing interpretation from the teacher. It is designed to be generic enough to apply to any standard:

Standard 5.1: Read chord symbols and interpret them by writing or describing the chord name and corresponding scale.

Advanced—The student meets or exceeds the standard.

Proficient—The student meets the standard most of the time (or meets most of the standard).

Developing—The student meets the standard some of the time (or meets some of the standard).

Not Proficient—The student does not meet the standard.

Playing Tests   Performance assessments, or "playing tests," are probably the most authentic and meaningful form of improvisation assessment. After all, if we're going to assess improvisation, we should assess *improvisation*.

Just don't try to assess everything at once. Instead, decide on a single standard or component of improvisation to assess. If a more comprehensive, summative assessment is required, record the improvised performances so they can be reviewed many times.

Whenever possible, allow students the option of retaking their improvisation tests. Since improvised music is intentionally different every time it is played, it is only natural that some performances are better than others.

Group assessments can quickly be converted into playing tests. During call-and-response exercises, the teacher merely designates a single student to respond. Some teachers prefer to do a few quick assessments like this each day, rather than doing all assessments at once.

Portfolios A portfolio is a collection of student work that shows progress and achievement over time. Any assessment, whether formative or summative, can be recorded and placed in a portfolio. An exciting possibility, and one that is becoming increasingly feasible, is to include audio recordings of each student's improvisations in their individual portfolio. While we usually think of a portfolio as something kept in a binder, it could also be kept on a hard drive, CD, or mp3 player. As an added advantage, keeping these recordings over time can provide teachers with a growing library of audio examples for future students to hear and critique.

Games With so many things to learn, sometimes teachers and students alike forget that improvisation should be fun. Most formative assessment activities can occasionally be morphed into games. (The best thing about this approach is that students eagerly help do the necessary preparations or even invent the games themselves.)

- When reviewing chord symbols or other material, do it in the format of a popular quiz show. Give extra "points" if students can both identify and play the answers.
- Have a friendly end-of-term competition between sections to see which group can play the most jazz melodies from memory (or by ear).
- Have a race to be the first musician to play a new riff by ear in all twelve keys.
- Have "blindfold tests," where students listen to unfamiliar jazz recordings and try to identify the song and musicians.
- Pass out kazoos and have a scat-singing kazoo test.
- Invite the students to challenge the teacher to a call-and-response contest over an assigned harmony or harmonic sequence. Give them a week to prepare patterns that might stump you; the teacher will probably slip up eventually, but only after students have been "tricked" into practicing patterns all week!

Writing Essay questions and research papers can compel students to fulfill items in Standards 7 and 9. It is a mixed blessing that jazz students tend to be creative individuals and quickly tire of mundane assignments. If writing is desired, why not challenge them to assimilate and communicate the same information by writing original liner notes for a historical (or fictional) jazz album? Many classic jazz albums contain examples of excellent writing for them to emulate.

If you are performing a jazz standard at the next concert, invite students to write and present a brief speech to the audience. Another option is to write a review of a local jazz concert for the school newspaper or your own jazz ensemble blog. In fact, if approached correctly, blogging (creating and regularly updating an online journal, or web log) is a great way to encourage writing while documenting all kinds of student learning.

As students listen to jazz music in rehearsal and on their own, have them occasionally write about what they are hearing. For best results, require very specific content for some of these writing assignments, and occasionally give students the liberty to express their experiences more creatively.

Student Self-Assessment   Any of the aforementioned methods can be assessed by the individual students in addition to the teacher. Self-assessment makes students more aware of (and responsible for) their individual progress, especially when it involves recordings. Listening to recordings of themselves improvising is a shocking experience for some students, but an absolutely essential part of learning to be a self-sufficient musician. Have students evaluate their progress by listening to recordings of their improvisation attempts at both the beginning and end of the year. Their improvement in this short amount of time can be tremendous.

Consider having students self-assess often, identifying goals and progress regularly, perhaps as part of turning in practice records.

CONCLUSION

By teaching a logical sequence of improvisational materials and choosing charts to reinforce that sequence, jazz ensemble directors guide their students toward important standards of achievement. Choosing assessment methods that meet the needs of the ensemble is another way to ensure that students reach those standards.

NOTE

1. Musical fundamentals: pulse and meter, internal rhythm, articulation, correct style, rhythmic interest, note choice, solo development, space, interaction, melody and phrasing, dynamics, special effects, overall shape, creativity, and emotional impact. These components are discussed in Chapter 9.

⑪

JAZZ IMPROVISATION RESOURCES

Rather than detail each of the numerous publications, websites, and other jazz improvisation resources now available, this chapter gives examples of the *types* of resources available to jazz educators today and suggestions for how they might be used.

GUIDES FOR THE JAZZ ENSEMBLE DIRECTOR

A number of books are designed as comprehensive guides for the jazz educator. These books include wide-ranging information, from seating diagrams and mouthpiece charts to rehearsal techniques and literature lists. The task of effectively administering a jazz program, especially when combined with responsibilities for a complete band program, involves an incredible array of responsibilities. It is probably impossible to know everything that is needed. Every director should have at least one of these books to consult regularly in teaching jazz.

Complete Guide to Instrumental Jazz Instruction, by John Kuzmich and Lee Bash (West Nyack, NY: Parker, 1984)

David Baker's Jazz Pedagogy: A Comprehensive Method of Jazz Education for Teacher and Student, by David Baker (1969; reprint, Van Nuys, CA: Alfred, 1989)

Jazz Educator's Handbook, by Jeff Jarvis and Doug Beach (Delevan, NY: Kendor Music, 2002)

Jazz Ensemble Director's Handbook, by John Berry (Milwaukee, WI: Jenson Publications, 1990)

Jazz Ensemble Director's Manual, by Richard Lawn (Oskaloosa, IA: C. L. Barnhouse, 1981)

Jazz Pedagogy: The Jazz Educators Handbook and Resource Guide, by J. Richard Dunscomb and Dr. Willie L. Hill Jr. (Miami: Warner Brothers, 2002)

The Teaching of Jazz, by Jerry Coker (Rottenburg, Germany: Advance Music, 1989)

FULL-BAND JAZZ ENSEMBLE METHOD BOOKS

In a manner similar to full-band method books, these books are designed for teaching mixed instruments in jazz ensemble. This type of resource provides rehearsal structure, clear curricular direction and a breadth of instructional activities (especially valuable for those who may feel insecure about their ability to guide jazz rehearsals). Full-band jazz ensemble method books include improvisation study as one portion of their content.

Essential Elements for Jazz Ensemble, by Mike Steinel (Milwaukee, WI: Hal Leonard, 2000)

Standard of Excellence Advanced Jazz Ensemble Method, by Dean Sorenson and Bruce Pearson (San Diego, CA: Neil A. Kjos Music, 2004)

Standard of Excellence Jazz Ensemble Method, by Dean Sorenson and Bruce Pearson (San Diego, CA: Neil A. Kjos Music, 1998)

FULL-BAND JAZZ IMPROVISATION BOOKS

These books provide in-depth improvisation instructional materials (including play-along CDs) designed specifically for use in the jazz ensemble class. While they may include other valuable information, these texts focus primarily on the development of improvisational skills.

Approaching the Standards (Jazz Improvisation Series), by Willie Hill (Miami: Warner Brothers, 2000)

Chop-Monster Jazz Language Tutor (Chop-Monster series), by Shelly Berg (Hollywood, CA: J. Fraser, 1998)

Jazz Basics: The Fundamentals of Improvisation for the Young Musician, by Peter Blair (Dayton, OH: The Lorenz Corporation, 2004)

COMBO RESOURCES

Understanding how to make music in the combo setting is valuable for all musicians in the jazz ensemble. Jazz musician Horace Silver's informative book on combos also includes charts for performance.

The Art of Small Combo Jazz Playing, Composing, and Arranging, by Horace Silver (Milwaukee, WI: Hal Leonard, 1995)

The *IAJE-MTNA Jazz Studies Guide* (Cincinnati, OH: Music Teachers National Association, 2001) includes both guidelines for mastering improvisational materials and a valuable list of jazz tunes that use standard harmonic progressions.

Fakebooks contain the melody and chord changes for many songs. They can be used directly to learn tunes or as a reference to supplement learning tunes by ear. In the past, fakebooks have generally been disseminated in violation of copyright laws, but now many high-quality and affordable legal books exist. The primary publishers of fakebooks are Hal Leonard, Sher Music, and Warner Brothers.

Hal Leonard's fakebooks include *The Real Book*, the *Ultimate Jazz Fakebook*, and the *Real Jazz Fakebook*.

Sher Music publishes an expansive variety of fakebooks, including *The New Real Book* and the *Real Easy Book*, each available in numerous volumes. Each *Real Easy Book* is marvelously designed for use by less experienced jazz students and includes instruction for constructing piano voicings and bass lines.

Warner Brothers publishes fakebooks including the *Just Jazz Real Book*, *Just Standards Real Book*, and *Just Blues Real Book*.

RHYTHM SECTION AND INTERACTION

Perhaps because the majority of the musicians in the jazz ensemble play wind instruments, rhythm sections tend to get less attention than they need. Because the rhythm section supplies the harmonic foundation, the fastest way to improve the overall sound and improvisation of most jazz ensembles is to improve the quality of playing in the rhythm section.

Chord Voicing Handbook, by Matt Harris and Jeff Jarvis (Delevan, NY: Kendor Music, 1994)

Guitarist's Guide to the Jazz Ensemble, by Jack Grassel (Miami: Jenson Publications, 1989)

How to Comp: A Study in Jazz Accompaniment, by Hal Crook (Rottenburg, Germany: Advance Music, 1995)

Interaction: Opening Up the Jazz Ensemble, by Graham Collier (Rottenburg, Germany: Advance Music, 1995)

Jazz Piano Voicings for the Non-Pianist, by Mike Tracy (New Albany, IN: Jamey Aebersold Jazz, 1998)

Music Director's Guide to the Drumset, by Frank May (Milwaukee, WI: Hal Leonard, 1992)

Rhythm Section Workshop for Jazz Directors, by Shelly Berg, Lou Fischer, Fred Hamilton, and Steve Houghton (Van Nuys, CA: Alfred, 2005)

Voicing and Comping for Jazz Vibraphone, by Thomas Davis (Milwaukee, WI: Hal Leonard, 1999)

PLAY-ALONG RECORDINGS

Jazz play-alongs are usually books with corresponding CDs that enable students to practice improvisation with a recording of a professional jazz rhythm section playing the harmonic background to various songs. Every student of improvisation should practice with harmonic accompaniment. Most of these recordings feature the bass and piano on different stereo channels, so that either one can be muted during playback if desired.

Hal Leonard Jazz Play-along, 77+ volumes (Milwaukee, WI: Hal Leonard).
   These include an optional melody track.
Jamey Aebersold Play-A-Longs, 124+ volumes (New Albany, IN: Jamey Aeber-
   sold Jazz)

Playjazznow.com is a relatively new resource that features play-along
recordings, available as single songs or collections, which may be down-
loaded for a fee.

PLAY-ALONG TECHNOLOGY

The following products provide play-along opportunities through technology. The advantage to using software is that an accompaniment to
any song can be generated by simply inputting the chord changes.
Tempo, key, and playback style can be altered easily. Differing styles of
playback are also possible, as are a multitude of other features. The dis-
advantage (one that is lessening somewhat over time) is that the quality
of sound does not equal authentic instruments and musicians.

Band-in-a-Box: www.pgmusic.com
MiBac Jazz: www.mibac.com

   Another possible resource for harmonic accompaniments is midi files
posted on the Internet. Midi files have the advantage of very small file
size, with the tradeoff of poor sound quality.

THEORY BOOKS

Jazz theory books are useful references for jazz educators, especially
since most books directed specifically toward educators do not contain
much theory information.

Chord Scale Theory and Jazz Harmony, by Richard Graf and Barrie Nettles
   (Rottenburg, Germany: Advance Music, 1997)
Jazz Harmony, by Andrew Jaffe (Dubuque, IA: William C. Brown, 1983)
Jazz Theory and Practice, by Richard Lawn and Jeffrey Hellmer (Los Angeles:
   Alfred, 1996)

The Jazz Theory Book, by Mark Levine (Petaluma, CA: Sher Music, 1995)

Jazz Theory Resources (Volumes 1 and 2), by Bert Ligon (Milwaukee, WI: Houston, 2001)

The Jazz Theory Workbook, by Mark Boling (Rottenburg, Germany: Advance Music, 1990)

Jazzology: An Encyclopedia of Jazz Theory for All Musicians, by Robert Rawlins and Nor Eddine Bahha (Milwaukee, WI: Hal Leonard, 2005)

Lydian Chromatic Concept of Tonal Organization for Improvisation, by George Russell (New York: Concept Publishing, 1959)

Scales for Improvisation: A Practice Method for All Instruments, by Dan Haerle (Miami: CPP/Belwin, 1975)

PATTERN BOOKS

Jazz pattern books contain melodic patterns to be played over common chord progressions. The intent is that a large number of patterns can be ingrained. The patterns should be learned in all twelve keys. Patterns books are a great supplement to learning by ear, but not a great substitute.

Improvisational Patterns (multiple volumes), by David Baker (New York: C. Colin, 1979)

Patterns for Improvisation, by Oliver Nelson (New Albany, IN: Jamey Aebersold Jazz, 1966)

Patterns for Jazz, by Jerry Coker, James Casale, Gary Campbell, and Jerry Greene (Lebanon, IN: Studio P/R, 1970)

Repository of Scales and Melodic Patterns, by Yusef Lateef (Amherst, MA: Fana Music, 1981)

Scales for Jazz Improvisation: A Practice Method for All Instruments, by Dan Haerle (Miami: CPP/Belwin, 1975)

Thesaurus of Scales and Melodic Patterns, by Nicholas Slonimsky (New York: Coleman-Ross, 1947)

GENERAL IMPROVISATION RESOURCES

Anyone Can Improvise (DVD), by Jamey Aebersold

The Art of Improvisation, by Bob Taylor (Sandy, UT: Visual Jazz, 2006)

Beginning Improvisation (multiple volumes), by David Beecroft (Berlin, Germany: David Beecroft, 2002)

The Beginning Improviser (first in series), by Ramon Ricker (Rottenburg, Germany: Advance Music, 1996)

The Blues Scales: Essential Tools for Jazz Improvisation, by Dan Greenblatt (Petaluma, CA: Sher Music, 2004)

Building a Jazz Vocabulary: A Resource for Learning Jazz Improvisation, by Mike Steinel (Milwaukee, WI: Hal Leonard, 1995)

A Chromatic Approach to Jazz Harmony and Melody, by David Liebman (Rottenburg, Germany: Advance Music, 2001)

Complete Method for Improvisation, by Jerry Coker (Lebanon, IN: Studio P/R, 1980)

Constructing Melodic Jazz Improvisation: A Comprehensive Approach for Beginning and Intermediate Levels, by Brian Kane (Cambridge, MA: Jazz Path Music, 2007)

A Creative Approach to Practicing Jazz: New and Exciting Strategies for Unlocking Your Creative Potential, by David Baker (New Albany, IN: Jamey Aebersold Jazz, 1994)

Creative Jazz Improvisation, by Scott D. Reeves (Englewood Cliffs, NJ: Prentice-Hall, 1995)

Creative Rhythmic Concepts for Jazz Improvisation, by Ronan Guilfoyle (Dublin, Ireland: Newpark Music Centre, 1999)

Cutting the Changes: Jazz Improvisation via Key Centers, by Anthony J. Garcia (San Diego, CA: Neil A. Kjos Music, 2006)

The Goal Note Method, by Shelton Berg (Delevan, NY: Kendor Music, 1990)

How to Play Bebop (multiple volumes), by David Baker (Van Nuys, CA: Alfred, 1987)

How to Play Jazz and Improvise, by Jamey Aebersold (New Albany, IN: Jamey Aebersold Jazz, 1967)

Improvising Jazz, by Jerry Coker (Englewood Cliffs, NJ: Prentice-Hall, 1964)

Inside Improvisation (multiple volumes), by Jerry Bergonzi (Rottenburg, Germany: Advance Music, 1992)

Intermediate Jazz Improvisation: A Study Guide for Developing Soloists, by George Bouchard (New Albany, IN: Jamey Aebersold Jazz, 2000)

Jazz Improvisation: A Pocket Guide, by Dan Haerle (New Albany, IN: Jamey Aebersold Jazz, 2003)

Ready, Aim, Improvise, by Hal Crook (Rottenburg, Germany: Advance Music, 1999)

The Ultimate Jazz Tool Kit, by Scott Wilson (Ephriam, UT: The Jazz Education Store, 2007)

LISTENING/EAR TRAINING

The Art of Hearing: Aural Skills for Improvisers, by Thomas D. Mason (Milwaukee, WI: Houston, 1997)

Ear Training for the Jazz Musician, by Harry C. Pickens (New Albany, IN: Jamey Aebersold Jazz, 1985)

How to Listen to Jazz, by Jerry Coker (New Albany, IN: Jamey Aebersold Jazz, 1990)

Jazz Ear Training, by Jamey Aebersold (New Albany, IN: Jamey Aebersold Jazz, 1989)

Jazz Ear Training: Learning to Hear Your Way through Music, by Steve Masakowski (Pacific, MO: Mel Bay, 2004)

Training the Ear for the Improvising Musician, by Armen Donelian (Rottenburg, Germany: Advance Music, 1992)

CHARTS

Hal Leonard and Warner Brothers are, by far, the largest publishers/distributors of jazz ensemble music. Some wonderful music is available from other sources as well.

Jazz at Lincoln Center programs include a wealth of performances, broadcasts, and the Essentially Ellington High School Jazz Band Competition. While aspects of the Essentially Ellington program are competitive, the core purpose is to disseminate the music of Duke Ellington. Each year, directors can obtain six Duke Ellington charts (exact transcriptions), a reference recording, and a number of other resources for little more than the normal cost of a single chart (www.jalc.org).

Some additional resources for finding high-quality charts, as well as combo resources, are listed here. Most of these sites have music that cannot be obtained elsewhere.

3-2 Music Publishing: www.3-2music.com

Kendor Music: www.kendormusic.com

Marina Music: www.marinamusic.com (Marina Music is a distributor specializing in jazz with a large inventory and a very user-friendly search page.)

UNC Jazz Press: www.arts.unco.edu/uncjazz/jazzpress (University of Northern Colorado)

Walrus Music Publishing: http://www.walrusmusic.com

JAZZ HISTORY AND APPRECIATION

America's Jazz Heritage (Smithsonian): www.si.edu/ajazzh

Introduction to Jazz History, by Donald Megill and Richard Demory (Englewood Cliffs, NJ: Prentice-Hall, 1984)

Jazz for Young People Curriculum, by Wynton Marsalis (Miami: Warner Bros., 2002)

Jazz Styles: History and Analysis, by Mark C. Gridley (Englewood Cliffs, NJ: Prentice-Hall, 1988)

Ken Burns's *Jazz*: www.pbs.org/jazz

A New History of Jazz, by Alyn Shipton (New York: Continuum, 2001)

Smithsonian Jazz: www.smithsonianjazz.org

Thelonious Monk Institute: www.jazzinamerica.com

University of Chicago Jazz Archive: www.lib.uchicago.edu/e/su/cja

University of North Texas Jazz Research: www.library.unt.edu/music/links/jazz.htm

MAGAZINES

Jazz Educators Journal (published by International Association for Jazz Education): www.iaje.org/journal.asp

Jazz Improv magazine: www.jazzimprov.com

ORGANIZATIONS

International Association of Jazz Educators: www.iaje.org

International Association of Schools of Jazz: www.iasj.com

Jazz at Lincoln Center: www.jazzatlincolncenter.org

MENC: The National Association for Music Education: www.menc.org

Smithsonian Institution Jazz: www.smithsonianjazz.org

The Thelonious Monk Institute of Jazz: www.jazzinamerica.com

MISCELLANEOUS LINKS

Jamey Aebersold operates the most comprehensive site for obtaining most jazz resources (except charts). Several useful publications may be obtained from his website at no cost (www.jazzbooks.com).

Free military band recordings are available by request through the individual branches of the military. Some branches have full jazz ensembles, while others support smaller jazz groups. In every case, the musicianship is superb. Most of these sites also contain audio clips, articles, and other jazz-related resources.

www.usarmyband.com
www.army.mil/fieldband
www.usafband.com
www.navyband.navy.mil
www.marineband.usmc.mil
www.uscg.mil/band

The Jazz Education Store distributes a number of products, most notably worksheets and flashcards for teaching jazz theory and improvisation (www.jazz-studies.com).

JazzStandards.com features a list of one thousand important standard jazz songs. For many of the songs additional information is posted as well, including musical analysis, musician biographies, history, and links to recordings of the songs, including corresponding fakebooks and Jamey Aebersold play-alongs (www.jazzstandards.com).

Part III

CATALOG OF JAZZ ENSEMBLE CHARTS

USING THE CATALOG

Improvisational content should be a prime consideration in the selection of jazz ensemble charts. Directors are most effective when they use charts that help them to teach and reinforce improvisation, and avoid charts that disturb a logical sequence of instruction. Unfortunately, the improvisational demands of jazz ensemble charts vary widely, and specific information regarding their content is largely unavailable.

A limited number of charts now correlate directly with particular improvisation or method books. These are useful but won't yet supply enough performance material for most jazz ensembles. Few organizations use charts from a single publisher or educational series exclusively, but instead draw from a variety of sources to best meet the needs of their students. Irrespective of the difficulty in doing so, directors must locate charts that aid in the improvisational development of their ensembles.

To provide some assistance in accomplishing this significant task, a catalog of jazz ensemble charts organized by improvisational difficulty has been provided. Since the teaching of standard jazz songs is, of itself, an essential aspect of jazz education and improvisation instruction, arrangements of jazz standards have been chosen. Songs connected with significant jazz bands (sometimes considered "big band standards") and artists are included along with more universally recognized standards.

The catalog consists of three sections. The first two sections are indexes that list the charts, providing basic, summary information, while the third relates specific improvisational content through a fakebook-style lead sheet for each chart in the indexes.

Using the indexes, educators can quickly locate charts and determine general improvisational difficulty. Then, after locating a potential chart in the index, they can inspect the exact improvisational demands of that chart by turning to the corresponding lead sheet.

INDEXES

Title and Arranger

Each of the two indexes contains a summary of each chart's content. The first index listing is alphabetical, to correspond with the order of the lead sheet entries for each tune. The second index listing is organized according to written difficulty level. Since most directors are more familiar with written difficulty, this is the initial criterion; improvisational difficulty is organized *within* each level of written difficulty.

The title of the chart is listed first, followed by the arranger. The original composer is not indicated in these summary indexes, but is listed later with the lead sheet entries.

Although it is important to know the original composer, charts are typically organized only by arranger in printed catalogs and online search engines. Some confusion occasionally results from this system. For instance, after ordering *Easy Minor*, by Davis from a publisher's catalog, one might expect to receive an arrangement of the classic tune by jazz icon Miles Davis. Instead, they would receive an unrelated original composition by Tom Davis.

Publishers

The next item listed in the indexes is the publisher (abbreviated as "Pub"). The publisher abbreviations used in the index are as follows:

- BH: Barnhouse
- BW: Belwin

- FJH: FJH (Frank J. Hackinson)
- HJW: Heritage Jazz Works
- HL: Hal Leonard
- JALC: Jazz at Lincoln Center
- J: Jenson
- K: Kendor
- MP: Musicians
- MX: Matrix
- S: Sierra
- W: Walrus
- WB: Warner Brothers.

Tempo, Key, and Style

Next are listed the elements of tempo(s), key(s), and style(s). These are notated just as they were written on the original score, except that some style markings have been reordered so that the basic style occurs first, followed by any qualifying information. For instance, "Fast swing" is listed as "Swing—fast." When a range of acceptable tempos was designated, only the slower end of the range is indicated. In the alphabetical index, the written difficulty of the chart appears under the heading "W" and is simply the publisher's assessment of difficulty. The difficulty of the chart's improvisational section (according to the Grading Scale set forth in Chapter 7) is listed in both indexes under the heading "I."

Improvisation Format

The last entry for each chart in the index includes an optional brief reference to a few specific improvisational materials that offer immediate relation to significant sequences and forms.

The term "modal," as used in the catalog, implies that the soloist uses a single harmony for an extended period of time and that a limited number of total harmonies are used. This umbrella covers some traditionally modal tunes, excludes others, and also adopts some tunes that are modal only in the solo section.

"Blues" refers to the blues harmonic progression rather than to a certain mood or even title. (Some charts that are called blues, like "Basin Street Blues," do not actually contain blues form.)

The ii-V-I designation was used if the improvised section contained at least one complete ii-V-I progression. (In the abbreviated indexes, the symbols are devoid of chord extensions, as these vary widely. The full symbol can be found in the lead sheet for each tune.) The ii-V-i ("i" instead of "I") designation refers to the minor mode version of the progression. A minor ii-V-i implies not only that the final chord is minor, but also that the preceding chords function within the minor mode.

Often, using a borrowed mode, a major ii-V-I resolves to a minor tonic. As these may be interpreted as either a simple circle of fourths progression or as a resolution to the chord of the borrowed mode, these occurrences have not received special mention. The less frequently used designation "ii-V" indicates those solo sections made up primarily of alternating movement between ii and V.

Both ii-V and ii-V-I patterns are indicated in the index function as predominant, dominant, and tonic chords (at least for a temporary key area). Numerous apparent ii-V-I patterns were not listed, despite movement by fourths that resembles ii-V-I patterns. These charts differed in chord quality and therefore function; they could also be considered simple movement by fourths.

At times even quasi-functional ii-V-I or ii-V-i patterns were still omitted, as in the arrangement of "Round Midnight" by Lewis. The initial measures of this arrangement are very similar to Barduhn's arrangement of the same tune. However, only Barduhn's chart is listed as containing an ii-V-i. The resolution to a minor tonic in Barduhn's arrangement completes the ii-V-i pattern, whereas no such straightforward resolution occurs in Lewis's pattern. They are functionally similar. Educators wishing to reinforce basic patterns would likely want to use Barduhn's arrangement, whereas Lewis's might be more appropriate for later study.

To further assist educators who are teaching ii-V-I patterns, the key of each pattern is indicated. The key indicated corresponds to the final chord of the pattern. Using this guide, an educator could readily choose charts using ii-V-I patterns in the keys of B♭ and E♭ for the first concert and then expand to include additional keys in subsequent performances.

When AABA or other similar forms are indicated in the index, the soloist improvises over the entire harmonic form of the tune, rather than just a portion of it. Many tunes in the catalog are built upon standard song forms, such as AABA, but students do not often improvise over the entire form. When a portion of the form is in parentheses, such as AA(B)A, the soloist does not improvise over the section in parentheses but benefits from being aware of the overall form. If the soloist improvises over only a small part of a standard form, the form has not been indicated. Since the information in the index is intended to relate to teaching improvisation, the guideline for labeling format was not "What is the form of the chart?" but "What are the changes of the solo section?"

Of course, many charts might have been interpreted differently. Tyzik's arrangement of "Children of Sanchez" contains eight measures corresponding to a blues form, more than some of the partial-chorus charts that are listed as blues. In this case, preference was given to the fact that soloists in "Children of Sanchez" do improvise over a longer form that involves significant *additional* elements beyond the blues form. On the other hand, the abbreviated solo sections of blues tunes contain elements of blues form *exclusively*.

"Rhythm" (short for *rhythm changes*) refers to the harmonic changes derived from the song "I Got Rhythm." Again, this designation is given only when the soloist improvises over the whole form, or a significant portion of it. Like the blues form, rhythm changes can include many alterations. Interestingly, the chart "I Got Rhythm," as arranged by Ford, is not listed as having "rhythm" for its harmonic content, because of an abbreviated solo section and considerable harmonic alterations.

LEAD SHEETS

Using the indexes, educators can quickly locate the title, arranger, publisher, tempo, key, style, written difficulty, improvisational difficulty, and selected improvisational elements of a chart. Because no summary can completely communicate the total improvisational demands of a chart, the final section of the catalog includes the exact chord changes of the entire improvised section, notated as a fakebook-style lead sheet. In this way, teachers can first use the condensed index to quickly survey charts.

Uniform terminology has been used whenever possible in notating the lead sheets and indexes. An understanding of the terminology allows catalog users to quickly understand the various elements included in each chart.

When the phrase "as written or ad lib" is used, a written solo is provided *in addition to* written chord symbols. If the phrase "as written or ad lib" is absent, the solo section consists of chord symbols only.

The chord symbols are written as they appeared on the original charts, with two exceptions. The symbol $G^\triangle$, because of its brevity and clarity, is used in place of the synonymous major chord symbols to indicate a major harmony. Other major harmony possibilities, including G6 and G6/9, are shown as they actually appear in the charts. For similar reasons, G- is used in place of Gm and Gmin.

At times the lead sheet appears to have a backward repeat sign going nowhere. In these cases, the corresponding forward repeat sign appears earlier in the tune than at the beginning of the solo section.

Diagonal slashes within the staff represent the beats in a measure. A blank measure with no slashes indicates a measure in which the solo rests—usually while the ensemble plays. These empty measures are included to more clearly show the form of a chart. A measure including slashes but no chord symbol is a continuation of the chord last notated. (Each chord continues until a new chord symbol is given.) The primary purpose of such notational practices is to succinctly express harmonic content and to make harmonic patterns more readily apparent.

Chords that change off the beat are adjusted to the nearest beat or to the beat of longest duration. An effort was made to visually line up phrases vertically (i.e., to draw attention to the repeated patterns of chords that often occur in four-, eight-, and twelve-measure segments). At times the density of a progression made it unwieldy to fit the desired number of measures into a single system. These phrases were typically divided, for instance, from eight measures in a system to four measures in a system.

The instrument for which the solo is intended is indicated on the lead sheet. "Opening up" the solo section for all students to practice is highly recommended. This approach requires very little adjustment and vastly enhances the effectiveness of time spent rehearsing improvisation. The lead sheets are an example of the kind of solo guide that should be distributed to every student in the band. Not only can all of the students then practice improvising, but also many of the other aforementioned improvisational exercises are facilitated. For instance, using the lead sheet as a reference, band members can devise their own harmonically correct backgrounds while a single soloist improvises freely.

Remember that the difficulty levels do not designate the *quality* of a solo section, simply the *difficulty*. Although disparity exists between the written and improvised difficulty in many tunes, this may actually prove beneficial. Matching written and improvisational difficulties are only preferred in the rare situation when students have had equal experience and instruction in written and improvised music.

Consider also that a significant contributor to difficulty is simply the familiarity of the materials. Educators may choose to follow a sequence of improvisational instruction different from the one suggested, resulting in some shifting as to which harmonies are most and least familiar. Using the lead sheets as a guide, they should still be able to find charts that support the sequence

Some charts are, but for the presence of a single harmony, much easier than their listed difficulty. They could be successfully navigated by a less experienced soloist if the soloist were given proper instruction. For instance, Sweeney's version of "Freddie Freeloader" largely aligns with Level 1, but then includes a diminished chord. In one sense, it may seem drastic to jump four grade levels due to the inclusion of two beats of unfamiliar harmony. In the same way, however, the written difficulty of a chart would be greatly influenced by a single high-range note or a brief but particularly challenging rhythmic or technical passage. (To rehearse "Freddie Freeloader" effectively with an inexperienced band, allow extra time for learning the diminished chord/scale, or instruct students to play a specific note or rest when the harmony occurs.)

While it has limited harmonic demands and infrequent changes of harmony, Sweeney's arrangement of "Caravan" is at improvisation Level 5 because it uses harmonic elements that are less common. It is to the student's advantage to focus early attention on the most common, consonant, and transferable types of aural and technical skills. When the time comes for the first experience with these slash chords, the format ought to be simple enough to enable the improviser to focus on the new sound and become adept at expression within it. This version of "Caravan" may be ideal for such a situation (if the band is also well served by playing a chart with a Grade 2 written difficulty).

A large number of jazz ensemble charts contain no improvisation at all. Some, like Murtha's "Milestones" arrangement and Barrett's version of "Opus One," do say, "Solo—as written or ad lib," but offer only a written solo, with no chords indicated. These must also be categorized as containing no improvisation, but may be effectively used to balance a concert program that already contains ample improvisational challenges.

Of course some people favor limiting improvisation opportunities— directors who use written solos exclusively or avoid improvisation altogether. Others may regularly feature the same few soloists. Perhaps these choices were prompted by improvisational formats that seemed beyond the reach of the ensemble as a whole. The information and resources in this book make it easier to obtain charts correlating with a logical sequence of improvisation instruction. Teaching improvisation and the charts in tandem promotes high levels of ensemble performance while simultaneously developing the individual improvisation skills of each student in the band.

Use the following activities to familiarize yourself with the catalog.

- Compare arrangements of the same tune, such as "Take the A Train," to find the version that best meets the written and improvisational needs of a particular ensemble. Consult the lead sheet to determine which part of the AABA form students improvise over. Notice whether the chords include extensions and alterations.
- Locate compositions that have a Grade 3 written difficulty, but only a Grade 1 improvisational difficulty. These charts would be ideal for instrumentalists with music reading experience but no improvisational experience. Consult the lead sheet in advance to see specifically what kind of harmonies students need to know for each chart.
- Locate any compositions that have a Grade 1 written difficulty but a Grade 4 improvisational difficulty. These charts could be ideal for showcasing an experienced soloist in an inexperienced band.

For convenience in searching the catalog, the scale of sequential improvisational difficulty is reprinted here, prior to the first index.

GRADING SCALE OF IMPROVISATIONAL DIFFICULTY IN JAZZ ENSEMBLE CHARTS

Grade Zero—No improvisation

Grade 1—Improvised sections contain no more than two total chords and only one chord type

- Major (Ionian) chords (C)
- Dominant (Mixolydian) chords (C7)
- Minor (Dorian or Aeolian) chords (C-7)
- Moderate tempo, common time

Grade 2—Improvised sections may contain any of the above, as well as the following:

- Changing modalities (major/Mixolydian/Dorian)
- Slow to moderate harmonic movement (rate of chord change)
- Major ii-V progressions
- Major ii-V-I progresssions
- Basic blues form
- Standard thirty-two-bar song form—AABA
- Moderate tempo, 3/4 time

Grade 3—Improvised sections may contain any of the above, as well as the following:

- Minor tonic chords (C-$^\Delta$7, C6/9)
- Half-diminished chords (C$^\emptyset$)
- Altered chords (C7^{ALT})
- Minor ii-V-i progressions
- Minor blues form
- Standard thirty-two-bar song form—ABAB, ABAC
- Moderately fast and slow tempo
- Cut time, 6/8

Grade 4—Improvised sections may contain any of the above, as well as the following:

- Diminished chords (C° and C♭9)
- Suspended chords (Csus)
- Augmented chords (C7+5)
- Lydian harmony (C△♯4)
- Lydian dominant harmony (C7♯4)
- Rhythm changes, bebop changes, Bird blues
- Challenging tempo and meter

Grade 5—Improvised sections may contain any of the above, as well as the following:

- Slash chords and bitonality
- All additional chords, including other forms of altered dominants
- "Giant Steps" and other advanced forms
- Extreme tempos and challenging meter

ALPHABETICAL INDEX OF JAZZ ENSEMBLE CHARTS

Title	Arranger	Pub	Tempo	Key	Style	W	I	Improvisation Format
Afro Blue	Mossman	HL	196	Bb	Latin—Guiro 6/8 feel	4	5	Blues: minor
Afro Blue	Sweeney	HL	80, 60	Bb	Latin—Afro Latin	3	4	
After You've Gone	Holman	S	240	Bb	Swing—fast swing, cool	3.5	5	
All Blues	Sweeney	HL	132	Bb	Swing—medium	2	5	Blues
Allright, Okay, You Win	Nestico	HL	140	Eb	Shuffle—medium	3	4	Blues
Allright, Okay, You Win	Sweeney	HL	112	F	Shuffle—bluesy	2	2	Blues
American Patrol	Holcombe	MP	160	Eb	Swing—fast 4	4	0	None
Angel Eyes	Foster, F.	WB	100	F	Ballad	4	4	ii-V-I (Bb)
April in Paris	Lowden, B.	WB	128	C	Swing—moderate	4	3	ii-V-i (A)
April in Paris	Sweeney	HL	112	Bb	Swing—relaxed	1	3	ii-V-I (Eb)
As Time Goes By	Denton, J.	WB	100	Bb	Swing—slow	2	4	ii-V-I (Eb, Ab)
Autumn Leaves	Berry, J.	HL	138	F	Swing	2	4	ii-V-I (F)
Autumn Leaves	Blair, P.	HL	144	F	Swing—medium fast	3	3	ii-V-I (F), ii-V-i (D)
Basin Street Blues	Jennings, P.	HL	96	Bb, Eb	Swing—Dixieland	3	4	ii-V-I (Bb)
Basin Street Blues	Sweeney	HL	96	Bb	Swing—moderate	2	4	ii-V-I (Bb)
Begin the Beguine	Hest, J.	WB		D, G	Swing—in 4	3.5	0	None
Big Dipper	Jones, T.	K	136	G	Swing—medium groove	4	4	Blues
Birdland	Higgins, J.	HL	160	Eb, F	Rock—fast	2	5	
Birdland	Kerchner	HL	156	F	Rock	3.5	0	None
Birdland	Sweeney	HL	152	F	Rock—fast	2	0	None
Black and Tan Fantasy	Berger, D.	JALC	77	Db, Bb	Swing—slow	3.5	0	None

Title	Arranger	Pub	Tempo	Key	Style	W	I	Improvisation Format
Chameleon	Sweeney	HL	88¢	Ab	Funk—moderate	2	2	ii-V (of Ab)
Children of Sanchez	Lopez, V.	WB	112	Eb	Latin—medium	3	2	
Children of Sanchez	Tyzik	WB	108	none	Latin—aggressive 4 beat	4	4	
Cool Joe, Mean Joe (Killer Joe)	Cooper, J.	WB	110	Ab	Shuffle—12/8 feel	3	2	
Cottontail	Berger, D.	JALC	234	Bb	Swing—fast	4.5	5	Rhythm
Cousin Mary	Murtha	HL	160	Bb	Swing—straight ahead	2	1	Blues
Cute	Custer, C.	WB	192	C	Swing—fast	3	5	None
Cute	Story, M.	WB	138	Bb	Swing—bright	2	0	None
Daahoud	Taylor, M.	HL	160	Eb	Swing—Bebop	4	5	ii-V-I (Ab)
Daddy	Bliss, J.	MX	140	Bb	Swing—easy	3	0	None
Dizzy Atmosphere	Yasinitsky	WB	160	Ab, Bb	Swing—Bebop	3	2	
Do Nothin' Till You Hear from Me	Berry, J.	HL	108	F	Swing—medium	3	4	
Do Nothin' Till You Hear from Me	Cook, P.	WB	104	F	Swing—moderately	2	2	ii-V-I (Bb, F)
Do Nothin' Till You Hear from Me	Jackson, J.	WB	142	Bb	Swing	4	4	ii-V-I (Gb, Bb)
Don't Get Around Much Anymore	Cook, P.	WB	126	Bb	Swing—moderate	2	2	
Don't Get Around Much Anymore	Ford, R.	WB	120	Bb	Swing—medium	2	4	
Doxy	Mills, D.	MX	120	Bb	Swing—medium	4	0	None

Title	Arranger	Pub	Tempo	Key	Style	W	I	Improvisation Format
Here's That Rainy Day	Curnow, B.	S	64	B♭	Ballad—straight 8ths	3.5	0	None
Here's That Rainy Day	Edmondson	HL	72	F	Swing—moderate ballad	1	0	None
How Deep Is the Ocean	Sweeney	HL	144	E♭	Latin	2	4	ii-V-i (C, G)
Hummin'	Barrett, R.	MX	96	F	Swing/ Funk Rock	4	2	
I Got Plenty o' Nothin'	Jackson, J.	WB	180	E♭	Swing/ New Orleans march	3	4	ii-V-I (E♭)
I Got Rhythm	Ford, R.	WB	144	E♭	Swing	2	4	
I Mean You	Dana, M.	MX	172	F	Swing/ Latin—medium-up	3.5	5	
I Remember Clifford	Vax	HL	66	E♭	Swing—slow ballad	3	4	ii-V-i (F, G)
I'm Beginning to See the Light	Goodwin, G.	HL	152	B♭	Swing	3	4	(A)AB(A),
I'm Beginning to See the Light	Taylor, M.	HL	120	B♭	Swing—medium	3	4	AABA
In a Mellow Tone	Berger, D.	JALC	134	A♭	Swing—medium	3.5	4	AABA
In a Mellow Tone	Cook, P.	WB	168	F	Swing	1.5	4	AA(BA), ii-V-I (B♭)
In a Mellow Tone	Sweeney	HL	116	B♭	Swing—moderate	2	4	AA(BA), ii-V-I (E♭)
In a Sentimental Mood	Dana, M.	HL	76	F	Ballad—even 8ths	3	0	None
In the Mood	Sweeney	HL	138	B♭	Swing—medium	2	4	ii-V (of B♭)
In Walked Bud	Berg, C.	MX	155	A♭	Swing—medium	4	5	
Isfahan	Mantooth	HL	152	D♭	Swing—medium	4	5	ABAC, ii-V-I (F, G)
I've Never Been in Love Before	Niehaus	S	72	B♭, G	Ballad—straight 8ths	3.5	4	ii-V-I (B♭)
Jada	Nelson, O.	S	70	F	Swing—slow	2.5	4	ii-V-I (F)
Jericho	Sharp, C.	FJH	144	F, A♭	Swing—1940s style	2	0	None

Title								
Jericho	Strommen	WB	126	F	Latin—lite	2	0	None
Jersey Bounce	Barrett, R.	MX	72, 150	Eb, Bb	Swing	3	4	ii-V-I (Eb)
Jive Samba	Clark, T.	MX	126	F	Latin—medium bossa	1.5	2	Modal
Johnson Rag	Wolpe, D.	WB	160	F	Swing—moderate	3	2	ii-V (of Bb)
Jumpin' at the Woodside	Cook, P.	WB	152	F, Eb	Swing—moderately fast	2	2	ii-V-I (Eb)
Jumpin' at the Woodside	Lewis, M.	WB	210	Ab, F	Swing—bright	3	5	Rhythm
Kansas City	Berry, J.	HL	126	Bb	Shuffle	2	2	Blues
Killer Joe	Higgins, J.	HL	126	Bb	Swing—medium	3	1	
Killer Joe	Sweeney	HL	120	Bb	Swing—medium groove	2	1	
Leap Frog	Berry, J.	HL	144	Bb	Swing	2	4	
Leap Frog	Cook, P.	WB	168	Bb	Swing—fast	2	0	None
Lester Leaps In	Taylor, M.	HL	180	Bb	Swing	4	4	Rhythm, ii-V-I (Bb)
Let's Dance	Blair, P.	HL	184	Eb	Swing—medium bright	4	4	
Li'l Darlin'	Hefti	WB	80	Eb	Swing	2	0	None
Li'l Darlin'	Phillipe, R.	WB	80	F	Swing	2	0	None
Little Sunflower	Owen, S.	MX	138	G	Latin	2	1	Modal
Mack the Knife	Nestico	WB	120	Eb, F, Gb, G, Ab, A, Bb	Swing—moderate	4	4	ii-V-I (F, Gb, G, Ab),
Maiden Voyage	Taylor, M.	HL	120	C	Latin—medium	3	4	Modal
Maleguena	Sweeney	HL	72, 144	Ab, Bb	Latin/Swing	3	4	Modal
Manteca	Owen, S.	MX	176	Bb	Latin	3	0	None

Title	Arranger	Pub	Tempo	Key	Style	W	I	Improvisation Format
Mercy, Mercy, Mercy	Wagoner	MX	112	Eb	Rock	2	2	
Milestones	Blair, P.	HL		F	Swing	2	1	Modal
Milestones	Murtha	HL	184	Eb	Swing—straight ahead	2	2	Modal
Milestones	Tomaro	HL	200	F	Swing—medium up	4	5	Modal
Minnie the Moocher	Ford, R.	WB	84	F	Swing—slow	2	0	None
Miss Fine	Blair, P.	HL	112	F	Swing—easy	3	5	
Misty	Mantooth	WB	168	Eb, F	Swing	4	5	AABA
Moanin'	Sweeney	HL	126	Ab	Swing—medium	2	5	ii-V-I (C)
Moanin'	Taylor, M.	HL	132	Ab	Swing—medium	3	5	
Moment's Notice	Taylor, M.	HL	184	Eb	Swing	2	5	ii-V-I (Db, Gb, Eb)
Mood Indigo	Nowak	HL	84	F	Swing—moderately slow	2	4	ii-V-I (F)
Moonglow	Cook, P.	WB		F	Swing—moderately slow	2	4	
Moten Swing	Sweeney	HL	120	Ab	Swing—medium	2	4	ii-V-I (Ab)
My Foolish Heart	Taylor, M.	HL	120	Bb	Latin—moderate bossa	3.5	5	ABA(C), ii-V-I (F)
My Funny Valentine	Taylor, M.	WB		Eb	Ballad—straight 8ths	3	5	
My One and Only Love	Taylor, M.	HL	56	C	Ballad—swing, double time	3	5	
My Romance	Taylor, M.	HL		Bb, Eb	Swing—slow ballad	4	5	ii-V-I (Eb), ii-V-i (G)
Nearness of You, The	Taylor, M.	HL	92	F, Db	Latin—soft	3.5	5	AABA
Never No Lament (Don't Get Around Much Anymore)	Berger, D.	JALC	116	Db	Swing—Medium	3.5	2	ii-V-I (Db)
Night in Tunisia, A	Ford, R.	WB	140	F	Latin/Swing	3	4	
Night in Tunisia, A	Sweeney	HL	160	Bb	Latin Rock/Swing	2	4	

Title	Arranger	Pub	Tempo	Key	Style	W	I	Improvisation Format
Sandu	Taylor, M.	HL	138	E♭	Swing—medium	3	2	Blues
Satin Doll	Edmondson	HL	100	B♭	Swing—moderate	2	3	AABA
Satin Doll	Nestico	HL	126	B♭	Swing—medium	3	4	AABA
Satin Doll	Taylor, M.	HL	112	B♭	Swing—medium	3	3	AABA, ii-V-I (F),
Shadow of Your Smile, The	Phillipe, R.	WB	72	A♭	Swing—medium	2.5	0	None
Sing, Sing, Sing	Cook, P.	WB	172	F	Swing—moderately fast	2	0	None
Sister Sadie	Dana, M.	MX	168	F	Swing—medium fast	2.5	3	Modal
Skylark	Wolpe, D.	WB	80	A♭	Swing—moderately slow	4	4	ii-V-I (A♭)
So What	Sweeney	HL	132	F	Swing	2	1	Modal, AABA
So What	Taylor, M.	HL	144	F	Swing—medium	3	1	Modal, AABA
Song for My Father	Taylor, M.	HL	144	A♭	Latin	3	2	
Somymoon for Two	Owen, S	MX	168	B♭	Swing—medium	1.5	4	Blues with a bridge
Soul Sister	Clark, A.	BH	120	B♭	Rock—funky tempo	4	2	
Sophisticated Lady	Wolpe, D	BW	72	A♭	Slowly	3.5	5	
Splanky	Custer, C.	WB	112	C	Swing—easy	3	5	Blues
Splanky	Phillipe, R.	WB	120	E♭	Swing—easy	2	2	Blues
Spain	Jennings, P.	HL	72	E♭	Latin—jazz samba	3.5	5	
St. Louis Blues	Davis, T.	HJW	162	F	Swing—bright	3	3	Blues
St. Louis Blues	Norred	FJH	112	F	Swing—medium	2.5	4	Blues
St. Thomas	Sweeney	HL	168	B♭	Latin	2	4	iii-VI-ii-V-I (B♭)
St. Thomas	Taylor, M.	HL	104	C	Latin—samba "in 2"	3	4	Cut time
Stolen Moments	Blair, P.	HL	108	F	Swing—medium blues	2.5	5	Blues: minor

Title	Arranger	Pub	Tempo	Key	Style	W	I	Improvisation Format
Things Ain't What They Used to Be	Mills, D.	MX	126	Bb	Swing	3	2	Blues
This Can't Be Love	Taylor, M.	HL	180	Ab	Swing	4	5	
Triste	Berg, C.	MX	125	Bb	Latin—bossa nova	3	5	
Tuxedo Junction	Berry, J.	HL	116	Eb	Swing—medium	2	4	
Until I Met You (Corner Pocket)	Taylor, M.	HL	144	Eb	Swing	3	5	AABA, ii-V-I (Eb, Ab)
Very Thought of You, The	Stone, G.	HL	60	Eb	Swing/double time	3.5	5	4/4 and Cut time
Walk, Don't Run	Rogers, S.	S	140	Ab	Swing—moderate	2	4	AABA, ii-V-I (Db, Ab)
When I Fall in Love	Carubia	WB	104	Eb, F	Latin—Bassa Nova	2.5	4	
When You're Smiling	Kubis	W		C	Swing	3.5	3	ii-V-I (C, F)
Woodchopper's Ball	Blair, P.	HL	168	Bb, F	Swing—medium fast jump	2	5	Blues
Work Song	Dana, M.	MX	160	Eb	Shuffle—medium (1/2 x feel)	1.5	4	
Yardbird Suite	Sweeney	HL	138	Bb	Swing—medium	2.5	4	ii-V-I (Bb)

INDEX OF JAZZ ENSEMBLE
CHARTS BY DIFFICULTY

Title	Arranger	Pub	Tempo	Key	Style	I	Improvisation Elements
Grade 1 (Written Difficulty)							
Blue and Sentimental	Phillipe, R.	B	60	Eb	Swing—ballad	0	None
Here's That Rainy Day	Edmondson	HL	72	F	Swing—moderate ballad	0	None
Night Train	Blair, P.	HL	94	F	Swing—medium slow	2	Blues
April in Paris	Sweeney	HL	112	Bb	Swing—relaxed	3	ii-V-I (Eb)
Black Orpheus	Murtha	HL	116	C, F	Swing	5	ii-V-I (C)
C Jam Blues	Stitzel	HL	126	Bb	Swing—medium	5	Blues
Grade 1.5 (Written Difficulty)							
Jive Samba	Clark, T.	MX	126	F	Latin—medium bossa	2	Modal
One O'Clock Jump	Cook, P.	WB	160	Bb	Swing—moderate	2	Blues, ii-V-I (Bb)
Harlem Nocturne	Blair, P.	HL	112	Bb	Latin/Swing	3	
In a Mellow Tone	Cook, P.	WB	168	F	Swing	4	AA(BA), ii-V-I (Bb)
Opus One	Barrett, R.	MX	192	Bb, G, C	Swing	4	
Sonnymoon for Two	Owen, S	MX	168	Bb	Swing—medium	4	Blues with a bridge
Work Song	Dana, M.	MX	160	Eb	Shuffle—medium (1/2 x feel)	4	
Grade 2 (Written Difficulty)							
Birdland	Sweeney	HL	152	F	Rock—fast	0	None
Boogie Woogie Bugle Boy	Sweeney	HL	152	Eb	Swing—bright	0	None
Cute	Story, M.	WB	138	Bb	Swing—bright	0	None
Jericho	Sharp, C.	FJH	144c	F, Ab	Swing—1940s style	0	None
Jericho	Strommen	WB	126	F	Latin—lite	0	None
Leap Frog	Cook, P.	WB	168	Bb	Swing—fast	0	None

Title	Arranger	Pub.	Tempo	Key	Style	Diff.	Notes
Li'l Darlin'	Hefti	WB	80	Eb	Swing	0	None
Li'l Darlin'	Phillipe, R.	WB	80	F	Swing	0	None
Minnie the Moocher	Ford, R.	WB	84	F	Swing—slow	0	None
Nightingale Sang in Berkley Square, A	Holmes, R.	HL	80	Eb	Ballad—straight 8ths	0	None
Now's the Time	Stitzel	HL	126	F	Swing	0	None
Perdido	Lewis, M.	WB	190	Bb, Eb, F	Swing—moderately bright	0	None
Rhapsody in Blue	Cook, P.	WB	80	Eb	Straight/Swing	0	None
Sing, Sing, Sing	Cook, P.	WB	172	F	Swing—moderately fast	0	None
Sweet Lorraine	Cook, P.	WB		F	Swing—slow easy swing	0	None
Cousin Mary	Murtha	HL	160	Bb	Swing—straight ahead	1	Blues
Killer Joe	Sweeney	HL	120	Bb	Swing—medium groove	1	
Little Sunflower	Owen, S.	MX	138	G	Latin	1	Modal
Milestones	Blair, P.	HL		F	Swing	1	Modal
Ran Kan Kan	Stitzel	HL	178	Bb	Latin—mambo	1	Modal
So What	Sweeney	HL	132	F	Swing	1	Modal, AABA
Allright, Okay, You Win	Sweeney	HL	112	F	Shuffle—bluesy	2	Blues
C Jam Blues	Cook, P.	WB		C, Bb	Swing—moderately fast	2	Blues
Caravan	Phillipe, R.	WB	160c	F	Latin/Swing	2	
Chameleon	Sweeney	HL	88	Ab	Funk—moderate	2	Optional cut time, ii-V (of Ab)
Do Nothin' Till You Hear from Me	Cook, P.	WB	104	F	Swing—moderately	2	ii-V-I (Bb, F)

Title	Arranger	Pub.	Tempo	Key	Style	Diff.	Form/Harmony
Georgia on My Mind	Sweeney	HL	88	E♭	Swing—bluesy	4	ii-V-I (E♭), ii-V-i (C)
Harlem Nocturne	Berry, J.	HL	88	B♭	Swing/Straight	4	ii-V-i (C, G)
How Deep Is the Ocean	Sweeney	HL	144	E♭	Latin	4	
I Got Rhythm	Ford, R.	WB	144	E♭	Swing	4	
In a Mellow Tone	Sweeney	HL	116	B♭	Swing—moderate	4	AA(BA), ii-V-I (E♭)
In the Mood	Sweeney	HL	138	B♭	Swing—medium	4	ii-V (of B♭)
Leap Frog	Berry, J.	HL	144	B♭	Swing	4	
Mood Indigo	Nowak	HL	84	F	Swing—moderately slow	4	ii-V-I (F)
Moonglow	Cook, P.	WB	120	F	Swing—moderately slow	4	
Moten Swing	Sweeney	HL	160	A♭	Swing—medium	4	ii-V-I (A♭)
Night in Tunisia, A	Sweeney	HL	132	B♭	Latin Rock/swing	4	
Opus One	Nowak	HL	152	F, B♭	Swing—moderate	4	ii-V-I (F)
Preacher, The	Edmondson	HL	168	F	Swing/2 beat: moderate	4	iii-VI-ii-V-I (B♭)
St. Thomas	Sweeney	HL	112	B♭	Latin	4	Blues
Swingin' Shepherd Blues	Phillipe	WB		F, B♭	Swing—medium	4	
Take Five	Lewis, M.	WB	154	E♭, F	Swing	4	ii-V-I (E♭), 5/4 meter
Take the A Train	Lowden, B.	HL	128	A♭	Swing—moderate	4	(AA)BA
Tuxedo Junction	Berry, J.	HL	116	E♭	Swing—medium	4	
Walk, Don't Run	Rogers, S.	S	140	A♭	Swing—moderate	4	AABA, ii-V-I (D♭, A♭)
All Blues	Sweeney	HL	132	B♭	Swing—medium	5	3/4 time, Blues
Birdland	Higgins, J.	HL	160	E♭, F	Rock—fast	5	
Blue Skies	Stitzel	HL	132	F	Swing—medium	5	ii-V-i (D)

Title	Arranger	Pub	Tempo	Key	Style	I	Improvisation Elements
Caravan	Sweeney	HL	108c	Eb	Latin/Swing—samba/½	5	Opt. cut time
Moanin'	Sweeney	HL	126	Ab	Swing—medium	5	ii-V-I (C),
Moment's Notice	Taylor, M.	HL	184	Eb	Swing	5	ii-V-I (Db, Gb, Eb)
Night Train	Higgins, J.	HL	104	Bb	Swing—easy blues tempo	5	Blues
Summertime	Custer, C.	WB	100	F	Swing—moderate	5	ABAC
Tenor Madness	Berry, J.	HL	146	Bb	Swing—medium	5	Blues
Woodchopper's Ball	Blair, P.	HL	168	Bb, F	Swing—medium fast jump	5	Blues,
Grade 2.5 (Written Difficulty)							
Shadow of Your Smile, The	Phillipe, R.	WB	72	Ab		0	None
Red Clay	Wagoner	MX	138	Eb	Rock—light	3	ii-V-I (Ab)
Sister Sadie	Dana, M.	MX	168	F	Swing—medium fast	3	Modal
Blue Monk	Sweeney	HL	104	Bb	Swing—medium slow	4	Blues, ii-V-I (Bb)
Jada	Nelson, O.	S	70	F	Swing—slow	4	ii-V-I (F),
St. Louis Blues	Norred	FJH	112	F	Swing—medium	4	Blues
When I Fall in Love	Carubia	WB	104	Eb, F	Latin—Bossa Nova	4	
Yardbird Suite	Sweeney	HL	138	Bb	Swing—medium	4	ii-V-I (Bb)
Stolen Moments	Blair, P.	HL	108	F	Swing—medium blues	5	Blues: minor
Grade 3 (Written Difficulty)							
Daddy	Bliss, J.	MX	140	Bb	Swing—easy	0	None
Fever	Holmes, R.	HL	138	C, Db	Swing—medium feel	0	None
In a Sentimental Mood	Dana, M.	HL	76	F	Ballad: even 8ths	0	None

Title	Composer	Publisher	Page	Key	Style	Level	Notes
Manteca	Owen, S.	MX	176	Bb	Latin	0	None
My Ship	Strommen	WB		F		0	None
Killer Joe	Higgins, J.	HL	126	Bb	Swing—medium	1	
So What	Taylor, M.	HL	144	F	Swing—medium	1	Modal, AABA
Blue Flame	Murtha	HL	76	Bb, Eb	Swing—easy and 12 feel	2	Blues
Children of Sanchez	Lopez, V.	WB	112	Eb	Latin—medium	2	
Cool Joe, Mean Joe (Killer Joe)	Cooper, J.	WB	110	Ab	Shuffle—12/8 feel	2	
Dizzy Atmosphere	Yasinitsky	WB	160	Ab, Bb	Swing—Bebop	2	ii-V-I (F)
Four Brothers	Blair, O.	HL	152	F	Swing—bright	2	ii-V (of Eb)
Groovin' High	Yasinitsky	WB	144	Eb	Swing—medium bebop	2	ii-V (of Eb)
Johnson Rag	Wolpe, D.	WB	160c	F	Swing—moderate	2	ii-V (of Bb)
Sandu	Taylor, M.	HL	138	Eb	Swing—medium	2	Blues
Song for My Father	Taylor, M.	HL	144	Ab	Latin	2	
Take the A Train	Berger, D.	JALC	165	C, Eb	Swing—medium	2	AABA, ii-V-I (Eb)
Things Ain't What They Used to Be	Mills, D.	MX	126	Bb	Swing	2	Blues
Autumn Leaves	Blair, P.	HL	144	F	Swing—medium fast	3	ii-V-I (F), ii-V-i (D)
Blues in the Night	Despain	WB	88	Bb	Shuffle—blues	3	Blues
Opus in Chartreuse	Murtha	HL		F, Bb	Swing—straight ahead	3	
Road Song	Dana, M.	MX	136	Bb	Latin	3	ii-V-I (Bb, Ab), ii-V-i (G)
St. Louis Blues	Davis, T.	HJW	162	F	Swing—bright	3	Blues
Satin Doll	Taylor, M.	HL	112	Bb	Swing—medium	3	AABA, ii-V-I (F)
Swingin' Shepherd Blues	Taylor, M.	HL	108	Bb	Swing—medium	3	Blues

Title	Arranger	Pub	Tempo	Key	Style	I	Improvisation Elements
Afro Blue	Sweeney	HL	80, 60	Bb	Latin—Afro Latin	4	3/4 time
Allright, Okay, You Win	Nestico	HL	140	Eb	Shuffle—medium	4	Blues
Basin Street Blues	Jennings, P.	HL	96	Bb, Eb	Swing—Dixieland	4	ii-V-I (Bb)
Black, Brown and Beautiful	Nelson, O.	S	76	Eb	Swing—ballad	4	ii-V (Ab)
Blue Bossa	Sweeney	HL	148	Bb	Latin—moderate	4	ii-V-I (Ab),
Blue 'n Boogie	Cook, P.	WB	144	Bb	Swing—medium up	4	Blues, ii-V-I (Bb)
Do Nothin' Till You Hear from Me	Berry, J.	HL	108	F	Swing—medium	4	
Easy Street	Barry, J.	HL	138	Eb	Swing—medium	4	ii-V-I (Ab, Eb)
Emancipation Blues	Holmes, R.	HL	72, 104	F	Swing—medium blues	4	3/4 and 4/4 time, Blues
I Got Plenty O' Nothin'	Jackson, J.	WB	180	Eb	Swing/New Orleans march	4	ii-V-I (Eb)
I Remember Clifford	Vax	HL	66	Eb	Swing—slow ballad	4	ii-V-i (F, G)
I'm Beginning to See the Light	Taylor, M.	HL	120	Bb	Swing—medium	4	AABA
Jersey Bounce	Barrett, R.	MX	72, 150	Eb, Bb	Swing	4	ii-V-I (Eb)
Maiden Voyage	Taylor, M.	HL	120	C	Latin:medium	4	Modal
Maleguena	Sweeney	HL	72, 144	Ab, Bb	Latin/Swing	4	
Night in Tunisia, A	Ford, R.	WB	140	F	Latin/swing	4	
Opus De Funk	Lopez, V.	WB	100c	B	Latin	4	Blues
Sack of Woe, A	Miley, J.	MX	90	Bb	Straight 8ths 1960s vibe/swing	4	Blues
Salt Peanuts	Despain, L.	WB	168	F	Swing—medium bounce up	4	Rhythm, AA(B)A
St. Thomas	Taylor, M.	HL	104	C	Latin—samba "in 2"	4	Cut time

Title	Arranger	Pub	Page	Key	Style	Level	Notes
Satin Doll	Nestico	HL	126	B♭	Swing—medium	4	AABA
Sugar	Clarke, T.	MX	124	E♭	Swing—medium	4	ii-V-i (C)
Take Five	Wolpe, D.	WB	160	A♭	Swing—moderately bright	4	5/4 time
Take the A Train	Barduhn	J	176	A♭	Swing—medium to fast	4	AABA, ii-V-I (A♭)
Take the A Train	Taylor, M.	HL	144	A♭	Swing	4	AA(BA), ii-V-I (A♭)
Blue Rondo a la Turk	Custer, C.	WB	112	E♭	Swing—brightly, moderate	5	9/8 and 4/4 time, Blues
Blue Trane	Taylor, M.	HL	152	E♭	Swing	5	Blues
Boplicity	Hooper, L.	WB	135	F	Swing—relaxed, cool	5	ii-V-I (A♭)
C Jam Blues	Pugh	WB	138	C	Swing	5	Blues, ii-V-I (C)
Cute	Custer, C.	WB	192	C	Swing—fast	5	
Doxy	Taylor, M.	HL	120	B♭	Swing—medium	5	AABA
Four	Talyor, M.	HL	152	E♭	Swing—Bebop	5	ii-V-I (E♭)
Jumpin' at the Woodside	Lewis, M.	WB	210	A♭, F	Swing—bright	5	Rhythm
Miss Fine	Blair, P.	HL	112	F	Swing—easy	5	
Moanin'	Taylor, M.	HL	132	A♭	Swing—medium	5	ii-V-i (F)
My Funny Valentine	Taylor, M.	WB		E♭	Ballad: straight 8ths	5	
My One and Only Love	Taylor, M.	HL	56	C	Ballad: swing, double time	5	
Round Midnight	Barduhn	WB	66, 52	F	Swing—slow	5	AA(BA), ii-V-i (D)
Round Midnight	Lewis, M.	WB	70	B♭	Swing—slow	5	
Splanky	Custer, C.	WB	112	C	Swing—easy	5	Blues
Stolen Moments	Taylor, M.	HL	108	B♭	Swing—medium groove	5	Blues: minor
Straight, No Chaser	Taylor, M.	HL	152	F	Swing—medium	5	Blues
Sugar	Taylor, M.	HL	120	E♭	Swing—medium groove	5	
Triste	Berg, C.	MX	125	B♭	Latin—bossa nova	5	

Title	Arranger	Pub	Tempo	Key	Style	I	Improvisation Elements
Until I Met You (Corner Pocket)	Taylor, M.	HL	144	Eb	Swing	5	AABA, ii-V-I (Eb, Ab)
Grade 3.5 (Written Difficulty)							
Begin the Beguine	Hest, J.	WB		D, G	Swing—in 4	0	None
Birdland	Kerchner	HL	156	F	Rock	0	None
Black and Tan Fantasy	Berger, D.	JALC	77	Db, Bb	Swing—slow	0	None
Early Autumn	Berry, J.	HL	80	Bb	Ballad: even 8ths	0	None
Here's That Rainy Day	Curnow, B.	S	64	Bb	Ballad: straight 8ths	0	None
Never No Lament (Don't Get Around Much Anymore)	Berger, D.	JALC	116	Db	Swing—Medium	2	ii-V-I (Db)
When You're Smiling	Kubis	W		C	Swing	3	ii-V-I (C, F)
Filthy McNasty	Labarbera, J.	K	130	Bb	Shuffle—medium	4	Blues
In a Mellow Tone	Berger, D.	JALC	134	Ab	Swing—medium	4	AABA
I've Never Been in Love Before	Niehaus	S	72	Bb, G	Ballad: straight 8ths	4	ii-V-I (Bb)
Rosewood	Lowden, B.	BH	176	Eb		4	
After You've Gone	Holman	S	240	Bb	Swing—fast swing, cool	5	
I Mean You	Dana, M.	MX	172	F	Swing/Latin—medium-up	5	ABA(C), ii-V-I (F)
My Foolish Heart	Taylor, M.	HL	120	Bb	Latin—moderate bossa	5	
Nearness of You, The	Taylor, M.	HL	92	F, Db	Latin—soft	5	AABA
Quiet Night of Quiet Stars (Corcovado)	Taylor, M.	HL	100	C	Latin—soft	5	
Sophisticated Lady	Wolpe, D	BW	72	Ab	Slowly	5	ii-V-I (G)

Spain	Jennings, P.	HL	72	E♭	Latin—jazz samba	5	Blues: minor
Stolen Moments	Jennings, P.	HL	108	B♭	Swing—moderate groove	5	
Very Thought of You, The	Stone, G.	HL	60	E♭	Swing/double time	5	4/4 and Cut time
Grade 4 (Written Difficulty)							
American Patrol	Holcombe	MP	160	E♭	Swing—fast 4	0	None
Doxy	Mills, D.	MX	120	B♭	Swing—medium	0	None
Groove Merchant	Barduhn	HL	116	E♭	Shuffle—medium groove	0	None
Round Midnight	Lopez, V.	WB	60	E♭	Straight/double time	0	None
Blues March	Mills, D.	MX	126	B♭	Swing—medium	2	Blues, ii-V-I (B♭)
Hummin'	Barrett, R.	MX	96	F	Swing/Funk Rock	2	
Soul Sister	Clark, A.	BH	120	B♭	Rock—funky tempo	2	
April in Paris	Lowden, B.	WB	128	C	Swing—moderate	3	ii-V-i (A)
Angel Eyes	Foster, F.	WB	100	F	Ballad	4	ii-V-I (B♭)
Big Dipper	Jones, T.	K	136	G	Swing—medium groove	4	Blues
Blues in Hoss Flat	Taylor, M.	WB	84	B♭	Swing—medium steam	4	Blues
Children of Sanchez	Tyzik	WB	108	None	Latin—aggressive 4 beat	4	
Do Nothin' Till You Hear from Me	Jackson, J.	WB	142	B♭	Swing	4	ii-V-I (C♭, B♭)
Early Autumn	Herman	HL	66	B♭, A♭	Ballad: even 8ths	4	ii-V-I (E)
Lester Leaps In	Taylor, M.	HL	180	B♭	Swing	4	Rhythm, ii-V-I (B♭)
Let's Dance	Blair, P.	HL	184	E♭	Swing—medium bright	4	
Mack the Knife	Nestico	WB	120	E♭, F, G♭, G, A♭, A, B♭	Swing—moderate	4	ii-V-I (F, G♭, G, A♭)
Skylark	Wolpe, D.	WB	80	A♭	Swing—moderately slow	4	ii-V-I (A♭)

Title	Arranger	Pub	Tempo	Key	Style	I	Improvisation Elements
Afro Blue	Mossman	HL	196	Bb	Latin—Guiro 6/8 feel	5	3/4 time, Blues: minor
Caravan	Tomaro	HL	112c	Ab	Latin/Rock—samba/swing	5	
Daahoud	Taylor, M.	HL	160	Eb	Swing—Bebop	5	ii-V-I (Ab)
Ellington Tribute, An	Berry, J.	HL	146, 76, 152 double	C, F	Swing	5	Blues, ii-V-I (C)
Fascinating Rhythm	Davis, T.	WB	172	Eb	Swing—bright	5	ii-V-I (Eb)
Georgia on My Mind	Nestico	HL	60, double	F, Db	Swing	5	ii-V-i (F)
In Walked Bud	Berg, C.	MX	155	Ab	Swing—medium	5	
Isfahan	Mantooth	HL	152	Db	Swing—medium	5	ABAC ii-V-I (F, G)
Milestones	Tomaro	HL	200	F	Swing—medium up	5	Modal
Misty	Mantooth	WB	168	Eb, F	Swing	5	AABA
My Romance	Taylor, M.	HL	—	Bb, Eb	Swing—slow ballad	5	ii-V-I (Eb), ii-V-i (G)
My Romance (Latin)	Taylor, M	HL	110	C	Latin—soft	5	ii-V-I (C)
This Can't Be Love	Taylor, M.	HL	180	Ab	Swing	5	

Grade 4.5 (Written Difficulty)

Title	Arranger	Pub	Tempo	Key	Style	I	Improvisation Elements
Groovin' Hard	Barduhn	HL	112	Eb	Shuffle—medium	0	None
Georgia on My Mind	Barduhn	HL	60	None	Swing—slow 12/8 feel	3	ii-V-I (F)
I'm Beginning to See the Light	Goodwin, G.	HL	152	Bb	Swing	4	(A)AB(A)
Things Ain't What They Used to Be	Lalama, D.	HL	132	F	Swing—medium	4	Blues
Cottontail	Berger, D.	JALC	234	Bb	Swing—fast	5	Rhythm

LEAD SHEETS FOR
JAZZ ENSEMBLE CHARTS

Afro Blue—Mongo Santamaria/Mossman
Tenor 1 solos the first time. After a D.S., Trumpet 2 solos, beginning at the third measure. The solo parts include suggested scales for each chord.

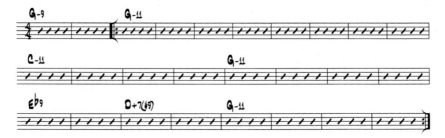

Afro Blue—Mongo Santamaria/Sweeney
Open solos. G minor pentatonic scale notated on all parts, but no chord symbols used. Written solos are included separate from the normal parts.

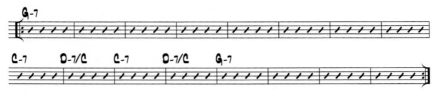

After You've Gone—Turner Layton, Henry Creamer/Holman
Trumpet 4

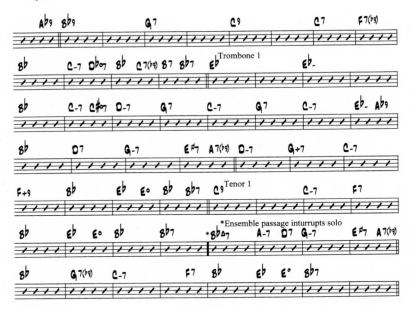

All Blues—Miles Davis/Sweeney
Trumpet 2 solo first time; Tenor 1 solo second time.

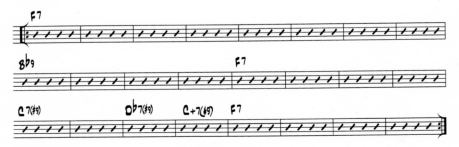

Alright, Okay, You Win—Sid Wyche, Mayme Watts/Nestico
The score indicates "open" solos. Alto 1, Tenor 1, and Trombone 1 have written solos in addition to
chord symbols. Piano and guitar parts have chord symbols only. No other parts contain solo material.

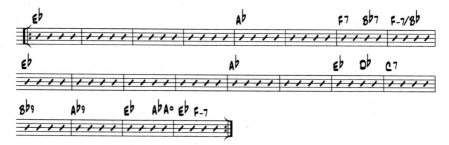

Alright, Okay, You Win—Sid Wyche, Mayme Watts/Sweeney
Alto 1 solo first time; Trumpet 1 solo second time. These seven measures are the end of a blues form.

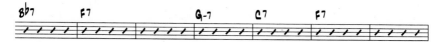

Angel Eyes—Matt Dennis, Earl Brent/Foster, F.
Alto 1

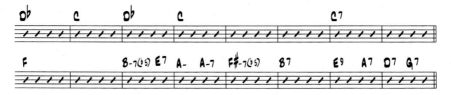

April in Paris—Vernon Duke, Yip Harburg/Lowden, B.
Trumpet 2 solo as written or ad lib.

April in Paris—Vernon Duke, Yip Harburg/Sweeney
Trumpet solo as written or ad lib. Written solo and changes appear in all trumpet parts.

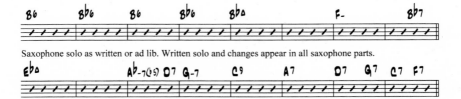

Saxophone solo as written or ad lib. Written solo and changes appear in all saxophone parts.

As Time Goes By—Herman Hupfield/Denton
Tenor 1 solo as written or ad lib.

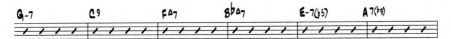

Autumn Leaves—Joseph Kosma, Johnny Mercer, Jacques Prevert/Berry, J.
Trumpet solo as written or ad lib. Written solo and changes appear in all trumpet parts.

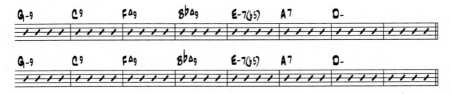

Autumn Leaves—Joseph Kosma, Johnny Mercer, Jacques Prevert/Blair, P.
Guitar solo as written or ad lib.

Basin Street Blues—Spencer Williams/Jennings, P.
Tenor 1 (optional clarinet), Trumpet 1, Trombone 1 solo simultaneously. As written or ad lib.

Basin Street Blues—Spencer Williams/Sweeney
Open solos. Separate written solo sheets.

Big Dipper—Thad Jones
Piano solo. Jones occasionally omits a measure of the form.*

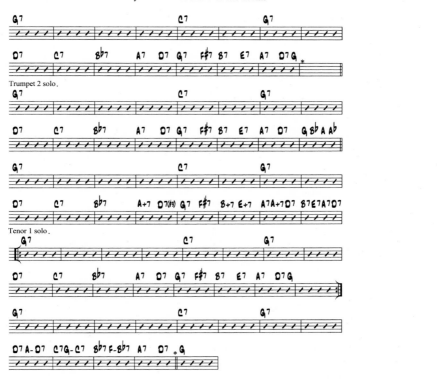

Birdland—Joe Zawinul/Higgins, J.
Alto 1 solo as written or ad lib. Repeat four times.

Black Orpheus—Louis Bonfa/Murtha
Trumpet 2 solo as written or ad lib.

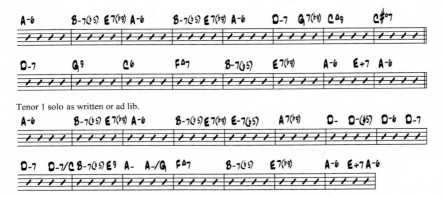

Tenor 1 solo as written or ad lib.

Black, Brown and Beautiful—Oliver Nelson
Alto 1 solo.

Solo pauses for ensemble passage.

Solo pauses for ensemble passage.
Final solo cadenza on D-11 chord.

Blue Bossa—Kenny Dorham/Sweeney
Trumpet 2 or Trombone 1 solo first time. Alto 1 or Tenor 1 solo second time. All solos are as written or ad lib.

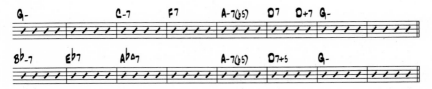

Blue Flame—Woody Herman/Murtha
Trumpet 2 solo as written or ad lib.

Alto 1 solo as written or ad lib.

Blue Monk—Thelonious Monk/Sweeney
Tenor 1 solo (optional Alto 1) as written or ad lib.

Trumpet 2 solo as written or ad lib.

Blue 'N Boogie—"Dizzy" Gillespie, Frank Paparelli/Cook, P.
Trumpet 1 solo as written or ad lib.

Alto 1 solo as written or ad lib.

Blue Rondo a la Turk—Dave Brubeck/Custer
Trumpet 2 solo as written or ad lib.

Alto 2 solo as written or ad lib.

Blue Skies—Irving Berlin/Stitzel
Solo for any saxophone as written or ad lib. Written solo and chord changes appear in all saxophone parts.

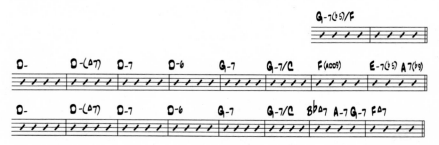

Blue Train—John Coltrane/Sweeney
Tenor 1 solo as written or ad lib.

Optional solo for Alto 1 or Trumpet 2. These parts have chords only (no written solo).

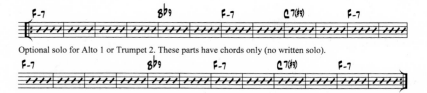

Blue Trane—John Coltrane/Taylor, M.
As written or ad lib solos for Trumpet 2, Tenor 1, Alto 1, and Trombone 1.

Blues in Hoss Flat—Frank Foster, "Count" Basie/Taylor, M.
Tenor 1 solo as written or ad lib.

Blues in the Night—Harold Arlen, Johnny Mercer/Despain
Each of the seven brief solos is as written or ad lib.

Blues March—Benny Golson/Mills, D.
Open solos.

Boplicity—Miles Davis/Hooper
Trumpet 2 solo first time; Alto 1 solo second time. Both as written or ad lib.

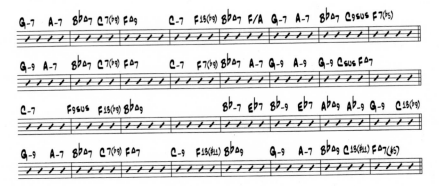

C Jam Blues—"Duke" Ellington/Cook, P.
Open solos are indicated in the score, and written solos are included in the parts. No chord changes are indicated in any of the parts. The following chord progression occurs during the written solos.

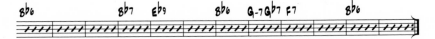

C Jam Blues—"Duke" Ellington/Pugh
Trumpet 2 solo first time; Tenor 1 solo second time.

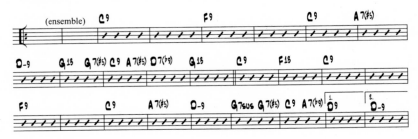

C Jam Blues—"Duke" Ellington/Stitzel
These solos each contain a partial blues chorus. The trumpet solo omits the first measure of the form. The sax solo omits the last measure of the form.

Trumpet solo as written or ad lib. Written solo and changes appear in all trumpet parts.

Saxophone solo as written or ad lib. Written solo and changes appear in all saxophone parts.

Caravan—Juan Tizol, "Duke" Ellington/Phillipe
Trombone 1 solo as written or ad lib.

Caravan—Juan Tizol, "Duke" Ellington/Sweeney
Solos occur during the samba section.

Tenor 1 solo.

Trumpet 2 solo.

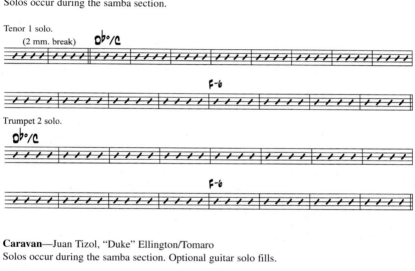

Caravan—Juan Tizol, "Duke" Ellington/Tomaro
Solos occur during the samba section. Optional guitar solo fills.

Trombone 1 solo.

Chameleon—Herbie Hancock/Sweeney

Alto 1 solo as written or ad lib. Trumpet 2 solo as written or ad lib also uses these same chord changes.

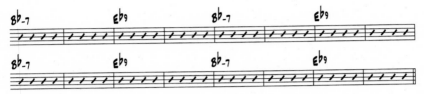

Children of Sanchez—Chuck Mangione/Lopez, V.

Open solos. Changes and written solos included in Trumpet 2 and Trombone 1.

Children of Sanchez—Chuck Mangione/Tyzik

Solo changes and written solos are provided for Alto 1, Tenor 1, Trumpet 2, and Guitar. Suggested scales are also written in each of the parts.

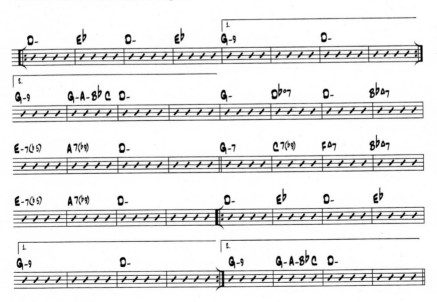

Cool Joe, Mean Joe (Killer Joe)—Benny Golson/Cooper, J.
Changes and written solos in Tenor 1 and Trumpet 2.

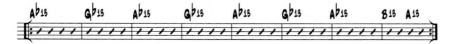

Cottontail—"Duke" Ellington/trans. Berger
Trumpet 1 solo as written or ad lib.

Baritone sax solo as written or ad lib.

Piano solo as written or ad lib.

Cousin Mary—John Coltrane/Murtha
Tenor 1 solo as written or ad lib. Trumpet 2 solo as written or ad lib over identical changes.

Cute—Neal Hefti/Custer
Tenor 1 solo as written or ad lib.

Daahoud—Clifford Brown/Taylor
Trumpet 1 as written or ad lib.

Dizzy Atmosphere—"Dizzy" Gillespie/Yasinitsky
Trumpet 2 solo first time; Trumpet 4 solo second time. Both solos as written or ad lib.

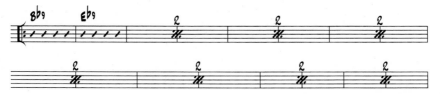

Four measures of ensemble follow,
then the section solo repeats

Do Nothin' Till You Hear from Me—"Duke" Ellington, Bob Russell/Berry, J.
Alto 1 solo as written or ad lib.

Trumpet 2 solo as written or ad lib.

Do Nothin' Till You Hear from Me—"Duke" Ellington, Bob Russell/Cook, P.
Trumpet 1 solo as written or ad lib.

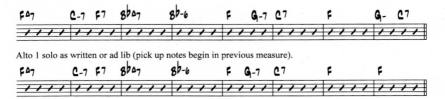

Alto 1 solo as written or ad lib (pick up notes begin in previous measure).

Do Nothin' Till You Hear from Me—"Duke" Ellington, Bob Russell/Jackson
Tenor 1 solo as written or ad lib.

Trumpet 2 solo as written or ad lib.

Don't Get Around Much Anymore—"Duke" Ellington, Bob Russell/Cook
Alto 1 solo as written or ad lib.

Trumpet 1 solo as written or ad lib.

Don't Get Around Much Anymore—"Duke" Ellington, Bob Russell/Ford
Trumpet 2 solo.

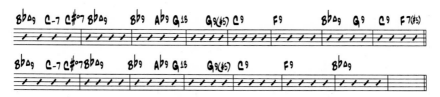

Doxy—"Sonny" Rollins/Taylor, M.
Open solos, ad lib or as written, in Alto 1, Tenor 1, Trumpet 2, and Trombone 1.

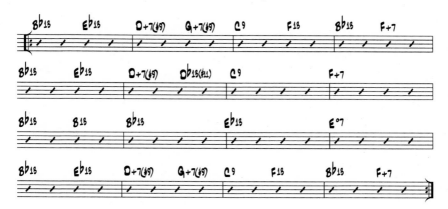

Dream—Johnny Mercer/Story
Trumpet 1 solo as written or ad lib.

Early Autumn—Ralph Burns, Woody Herman, Johnny Mercer/Herman
Tenor 1 solo as written or ad lib. This chart also contains a transcribed Alto 1 solo without chord changes.

Piano solo as written or ad lib.

Easy Money—Benny Carter/Sweeney
Trumpet 2 solo as written or ad lib.

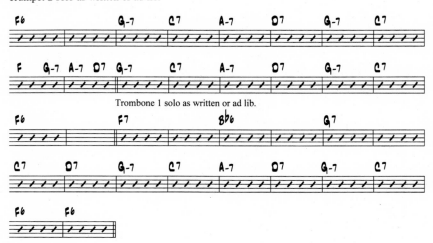

Easy Street—Alan R. Jones/Barry, J.
Trumpet 2 solo as written or ad lib.

An Ellington Tribute—"Duke" Ellington, Billy Strayhorn, Irving Mills, Mitchell Parish/Berry, J.
Includes portions of *C-Jam Blues*, *Sophisticated Lady*, and *Take the A Train*. Solos on *C-Jam Blues*:
Tenor 1 solo first time (24 measures); Trombone 1 and Alto 1 solo (each 12 measures) second time.
All solos as written or ad lib.

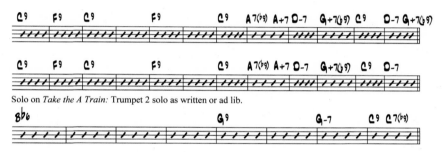

Solo on *Take the A Train:* Trumpet 2 solo as written or ad lib.

Emancipation Blues—Oliver Nelson/Holmes
Alto 1 or Trumpet 2 solo as written or ad lib.

Fascinating Rhythm—George Gershwin, Ira Gershwin/Davis, T.

Tenor 1 solo first time; Trumpet 2 solo second time. Both solos as written or ad lib.

The following (optional) additional open solo section occurs later in the chart with chord changes written in the Trumpet 2 part.

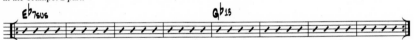

Filthy McNasty—Horace Silver/LaBarbera, J.

Alto 1 solo repeated three times. Trumpet 1 solo repeated three times.

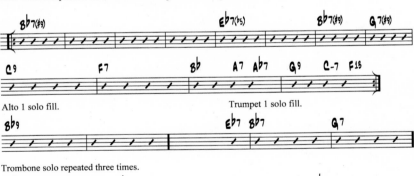

Alto 1 solo fill.   Trumpet 1 solo fill.

Trombone solo repeated three times.

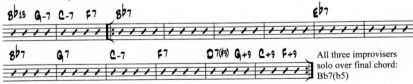

All three improvisers
solo over final chord:
Bb7(b5)

Four—Miles Davis/Taylor, M.
Tenor 1 solo as written or ad lib.

Trumpet 2 solo as written or ad lib.

Four Brothers—James Guiffre/Blair, O.
Optional open solo for any saxophone as written or ad lib.

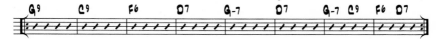

Freddie Freeloader—Miles Davis/Sweeney
Alto 1 solo as written or ad lib.

Trumpet 2 solo as written or ad lib.

Georgia on My Mind—Hoagy Charmichael, Stuart Gorrell/Barduhn
Alto 1 solo as written or ad lib. (Alto 1 also plays a written melody line solo that includes chord changes.)

Georgia on My Mind—Hoagy Charmichael, Stuart Gorrell/Nestico
Alto 1 solo. (Alto 1 also plays a written melody line solo that includes chord changes.)

Georgia on My Mind—Hoagy Charmichael, Stuart Gorrell/Sweeney
Unison written soli for Altos and Tenors or ad lib solo for any Alto or Tenor.

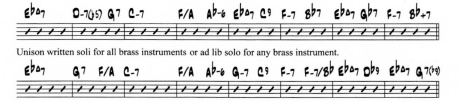

Unison written soli for all brass instruments or ad lib solo for any brass instrument.

Groovin' High—"Dizzy" Gillespie/Yasinitsky
Tenor 1 solo first time; Trumpet 2 solo second time. Both solos as written or ad lib.

Harlem Nocturne—Earl Hagen, Dick Rogers/Berry, J.
Alto 1 solo as written or ad lib.

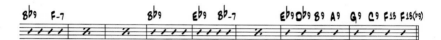

Harlem Nocturne—Earl Hagen, Dick Rogers/Blair, P.
Alto 1 solo first time; Trumpet 1 solo second time. Both solos as written or ad lib.

How Deep Is the Ocean—Irving Berlin/Sweeney
Tenor 1 solo as written or ad lib.

Hummin'—Nat Adderley/Barret
Tenor 1 solo first time; Trumpet 1 solo second time. Both solos as written or ad lib. Solos occur during the double-time swing section.

I Got Plenty O' Nothin'—George Gershwin, Dubose Heyward/Jackson, J.
Alto 1 solo as written or ad lib.

Tenor 1 solo as written or ad lib.

I Got Rhythm—George Gershwin, Ira Gershwin/Ford
Trumpet 1 solo as written or ad lib.

Alto 1 solo as written or ad lib.

I Mean You—Coleman Hawkins, Thelonious Monk/Dana
Piano solo first time; Trumpet 2 solo second time. Chord changes also written in Alto 1.

Additional Trumpet 2 solo repeated three times.

I Remember Clifford—Benny Golson/Vax
Trumpet 1 solo as written or ad lib.

Trumpet 1 also has cadenza solos on Major7 chords: Eb, Ab, and Eb(9).

I'm Beginning to See the Light—Harry James, "Duke" Ellington, Johnny Hodges, Don George/Goodwin
Alto 1 solo as written or ad lib.

I'm Beginning to See the Light—"Duke" Ellington, Johnny Hodges, Harry James, Don George/Taylor, M.
Alto 1 solo first time; Trumpet 2 solo second time. Changes are also given in Trombone 1 and Tenor 1.

In a Mellow Tone—"Duke" Ellington, Milt Gabler/trans. Berger
Trumpet 2 solo as written or ad lib.

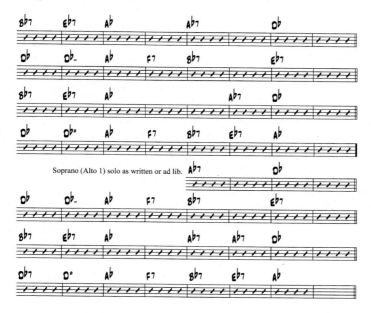

Soprano (Alto 1) solo as written or ad lib.

In a Mellow Tone—"Duke" Ellington, Milt Gabler/Cook, P.
Trumpet 1 solo as written or ad lib.

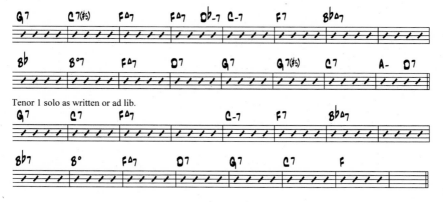

Tenor 1 solo as written or ad lib.

In a Mellow Tone—"Duke" Ellington, Milt Gabler/Sweeney
Unison written soli for all brass instruments, or ad lib solo for any brass instrument.

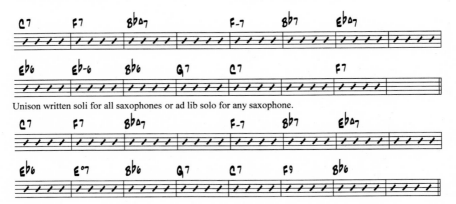

Unison written soli for all saxophones or ad lib solo for any saxophone.

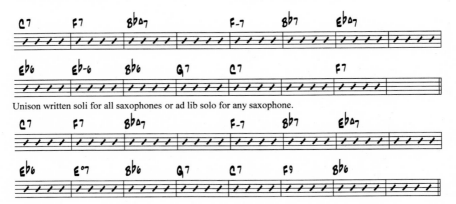

In the Mood—Joseph Garland, Andy Razaf/Sweeney
Alto 1 solo first time; Tenor 1 solo second time. Both solos as written or ad lib.

In Walked Bud—Thelonious Monk/Berg
Alto 1 or Trumpet 2 solo as written or ad lib.

Isfahan—"Duke" Ellington, Billy Strayhorn/Mantooth
Trumpet 4 solo as written or ad lib. All other parts have changes for open solos, but no written solo.

I've Never Been in Love Before—Frank Loesser, Paul Harris/Niehaus
Trumpet 4 solo. (Trumpet 4 also plays a written melody line solo that includes chord changes.)

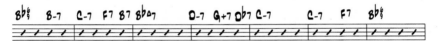

Jada—Bob Carleton/Nelson, O.
Piano solo.

Open solos (changes for each instrument are on separate solo parts).

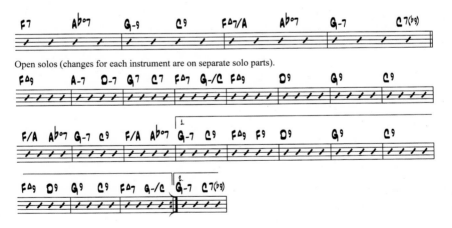

Jersey Bounce—Tiny Bradshaw, Edward Johnson, Bobby Plater, Robert B. Wright, Buddy Feyne/Barrett

Piano solo written with changes. (tempo = 72)

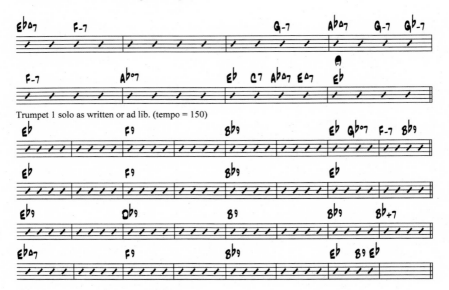

Trumpet 1 solo as written or ad lib. (tempo = 150)

Jive Samba—Nat Adderley/Clark, T.

Alto 1 solo as written or ad lib.

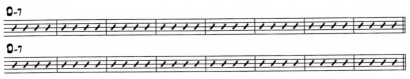

Trumpet 2 solo as written or ad lib. The Trumpet 2 part indicates G7 for 16 measures, however, the rhythm section outlines the chords as follows.

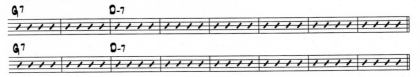

Johnson Rag—Jack Lawrence, Guy Hall, Henry Kleinkauf/Wolpe

Tenor 1 solo as written or ad lib.

Jumpin' at the Woodside—"Count" Basie/Cook, P.
Trumpet 1 solo first time; Alto 1 solo second time. Both solos as written or ad lib. Optional open for solos.

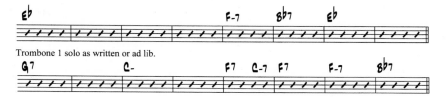

Trombone 1 solo as written or ad lib.

Jumpin' at the Woodside—"Count" Basie/Lewis, M.
Tenor 1 solo.

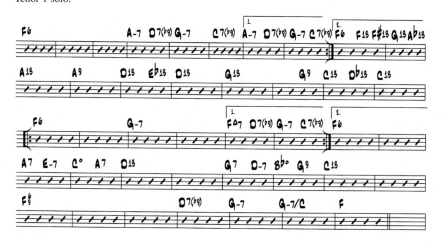

Kansas City—Jerry Leiber, Mike Stoller/Berry, J.
Alto 1 solo as written or ad lib. Trumpet 2 also solos as written or ad lib over same chord changes.
(Solo changes are measures 5–11 of the song's "12 bar blues" progression.)

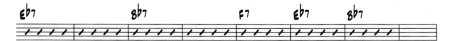

Killer Joe—Benny Golson/Higgins
Trumpet 2 solo as written or ad lib. Optional repeat for additional solos.

Killer Joe—Benny Golson/Sweeney
Written solo or ad lib for any saxophone. Written solo or ad lib for any brass over same chord changes.

Leap Frog—Joe Garland, Leo Corday/Berry
Written solo or ad lib for Alto 1 or any other saxophone.

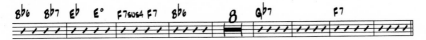

Lester Leaps In—Lester Young/Taylor, M.
Open solos.

Let's Dance—Gregory Stone, Joseph Bonine, Fanny Baldridge/Blair
Written solo or ad lib for any Alto or Tenor.

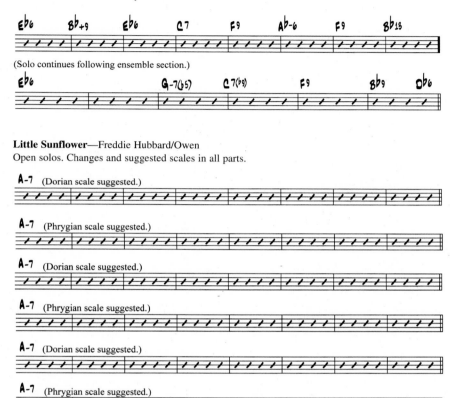

(Solo continues following ensemble section.)

Little Sunflower—Freddie Hubbard/Owen
Open solos. Changes and suggested scales in all parts.

Mack the Knife—Kurt Weill, Marc Blitzstein, Eugen Brecht/Nestico
Piano written solo with chord changes.

Trumpet 2 solo as written or ad lib.

Guitar solo (optional Trombone 1).

Maiden Voyage—Herbie Hancock/Taylor, M.
Open solos indicated. Changes are written only in Tenor 1 part.

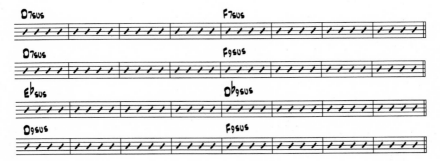

Malaguena—Ernesto Lecuona, "Dizzy" Gillespie/Sweeney
Solo for any trumpet first time, any saxophone second time. Solos as written or ad lib. Nonstandard
scale notated on all solo parts.

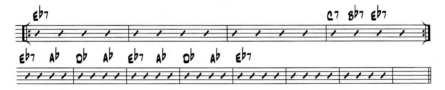

Mercy, Mercy, Mercy—Josef Zawinul/Wagoner
Alto 1 solo.

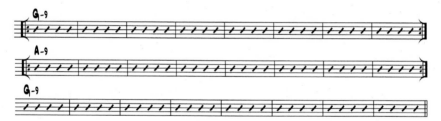

Milestones—Miles Davis/Blair
Open solos. Written solos and changes provided separate from regular parts.

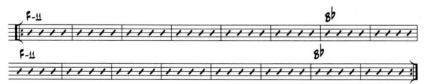

Milestones—Miles Davis/Murtha
Though the Tenor 1 and Alto 1 solos indicate "as written or ad lib," no chord changes are provided
for the soloist(s). The chord changes that correspond to the written solo are shown below.

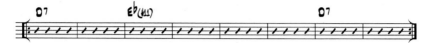

Milestones—Miles Davis/Tomaro
Trumpet 2 solo as written or ad lib.

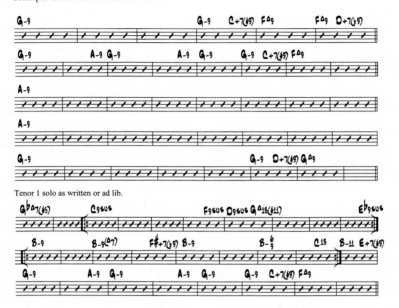

Tenor 1 solo as written or ad lib.

Miss Fine—Oliver Nelson/Blair
Trumpet 1 solo as written or ad lib.

Trumpet 1 additional solo.

Misty—Erroll Garner, Johnny Burke/Mantooth
Alto 1, Trombone 2, or Trumpet 4 solo.

Moanin'—Jon Hendricks, Bobby Timmons/Sweeney
Trumpet solo as written or ad lib (any trumpet). Individual parts indicate that the chord is F-6 for the duration of the solo. The actual chord progression is shown below. The Alto 1 part also indicates only one chord during the solo.

Moanin'—Jon Hendricks, Bobby Timmons/Taylor
Tenor 1 or Trumpet 2 solo as written or ad lib. Optional open solos.

Moment's Notice—John Coltrane/Taylor
Tenor 1 or Trumpet 2 solo as written or ad lib.

Mood Indigo—Barney Bigard, E. K. "Duke" Ellington, Irving Mills/Nowak
Piano solo (written) with changes.

Moonglow—Eddie DeLange, Will Hudson, Irving Mills/Cook, P.
Tenor 1 solo as written or ad lib.

Moten Swing—Buster Moten, Bennie Moten/Sweeney
Written or ad lib solo for any saxophone.

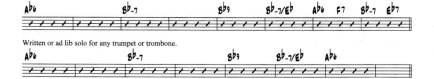

Written or ad lib solo for any trumpet or trombone.

My Foolish Heart—Victor Young, Ned Washington/Taylor, M.
Flugel horn solo as written or ad lib.

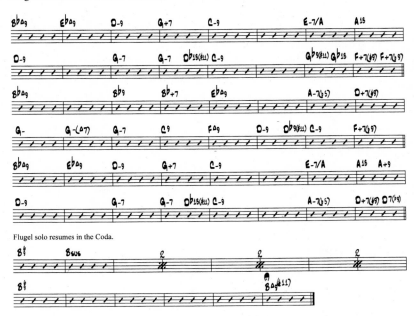

Flugel solo resumes in the Coda.

My Funny Valentine—Richard Rogers, Lorenz Hart/Taylor, M.
Tenor 1 solo as written or ad lib. (Solo is during samba section.)

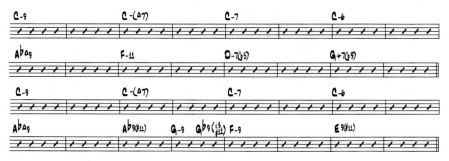

My One and Only Love—Guy Wood, Robert Mellin/Taylor
Alto 1 solo as written or ad lib.

My Romance—Richard Rogers, Lorenz Hart/Taylor
Trumpet 2 solo as written or ad lib.

My Romance (*Latin*)—Richard Rogers, Lorenz Hart/Taylor
Trumpet 2 solo as written or ad lib.

The Nearness of You—Hoagy Charmichael, Ned Washington/Taylor

Never No Lament (Don't Get Around Much Anymore)—"Duke" Ellington, Bob Russell/trans. Berger

A Night in Tunisia—"Dizzy" Gillespie, Frank Paparelli, Jon Hendricks/Ford, R.
Trumpet 1 solo as written or ad lib.

A Night in Tunisia—"Dizzy" Gillespie, Frank Paparelli, Jon Hendricks/Sweeney
Trumpet 2 solo first time; Alto 1 solo second time. Both solos as written or ad lib.

Night Train—Oscar Washington, Lewis Simpkins, Jimmie Forrest/Blair
Solo as written or ad lib in Alto 1, Alto 2, and any trumpet.

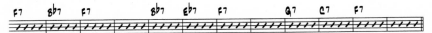

Night Train—Oscar Washington, Lewis Simpkins, Jimmie Forrest/Higgins
Trumpet 2 solo as written or ad lib.

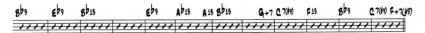

One O'Clock Jump—"Count" Basie/Cook, P.
Open solos. Changes and written solos provided on separate sheets.

Opus de Funk—Horace Silver/Lopez, V.
Alto 1 solo first time; Trumpet 2 solo second time. Both solos are as written or ad lib. Optional open solos.

Opus in Chartreuse—Gene Roland/Murtha
Alto 1 solo as written or ad lib.

Opus One—Sy Oliver, Sid Garris/Barrett
Trumpet 1 solo first time; Tenor sax 1 solo second time. Both solos indicate as written or ad lib but provide the soloists only with the written solo (no chord changes). The actual chord changes of the solo section are as follows.

Opus One—Sy Oliver, Sid Garris/Nowak
Solo as written or ad lib for any trumpet first time, any trombone second time.

Solo as written or ad lib for any saxophone.

The Preacher—Horace Silver/Edmondson

Written piano solo with changes.

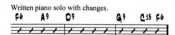

Solo for any saxophone first time, any trumpet second time. All solos as written or ad lib.

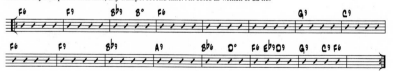

Quiet Night of Quiet Stars (Corcovado)—Antonio C. Jobim/Taylor, M.
Tenor 1 solo as written or ad lib.

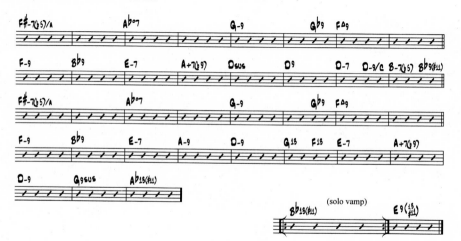

Ran Kan Kan—Tito Puente/Stitzel
Tenor 1 solo as written or ad lib.

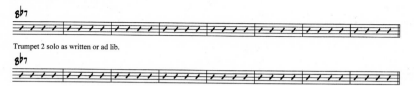

Trumpet 2 solo as written or ad lib.

Red Clay—Freddie Hubbard/Wagoner

Trumpet 2 improvises an introductory cadenza on C-7. Tenor 1 improvises a cadenza on A♭13. Then both soloists improvise simultaneously over two additional cadenzas: G7 (#9 ♭13) and C-7.

Tenor 1 solo first time; Trumpet 2 solo second time.

Road Song—Wes Montgomery/Dana

Trombone 1 solo first time; Tenor 1 solo second time.

Rosewood—Woody Shaw/Lowden

Tenor 1 solo first time; Trumpet 2 solo second time. Both solos as written or ad lib.

Round Midnight—Cootie Williams, Thelonious Monk, Bernie Hanighen/Barduhn
Trumpet 2 solo as written or ad lib.

D-7		E-7(b5)	A7(b9)	D-	G13	Bb-7 Eb7	A-7 D7
G-7	C13	D-7	G13	Bb7		A7	
D-7	B-7(b5)	E-7(b5)	A7(b9)	D-7	G13	Bb-7 Eb7	A-7 D7
G-7	C13	D-7	G13(b5)	Bb7	E-7(b5)/A	A7(b9)	D-7

Round Midnight—Cootie Williams, Thelonious Monk, Bernie Hanighen/Lewis, M.
Alto 1 solo as written or ad lib.

| G-6 | G-7/F | E-7(b5) | A-7(b5) D7(b9) | G-7 | C9 | Eb-7 Ab7 | D-7 G7 |
| C-7 | F7 | G-7 | C9 | Eb9 | D7(b9) | G- | |

A Sack of Woe—"Cannonball" Adderley/Miley
Solo for Tenor, Trumpet 3, or Trombone 1. Swing feel for all solos.

Trumpet 3 solo.

Salt Peanuts—"Dizzy" Gillespie, Kenny Clarke/DeSpain
Trumpet 2 solo as written or ad lib.

Sandu—Clifford Brown/Taylor, M.
Trumpet 2 solo first time; Tenor 1 solo second time. Both solos as written or ad lib.

Satin Doll—"Duke" Ellington, Billy Strayhorn, Johnny Mercer/Edmondson
Solo for any trumpet as written or ad lib.

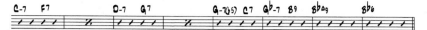

Satin Doll—"Duke" Ellington, Billy Strayhorn, Johnny Mercer/Nestico
Written piano solo with changes.

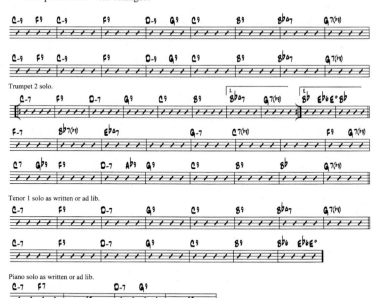

Satin Doll—"Duke" Ellington, Billy Strayhorn, Johnny Mercer/Taylor, M.
Open solos. Changes and written solos provided on separate sheets.

Sister Sadie—Horace Silver/Dana
Open solos.

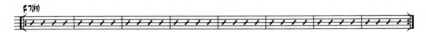

Skylark—Hoagy Charmichael, Johnny Mercer/Wolpe
Tenor 1 solo written melody with changes and the suggestion to embellish the melody.

Tenor 1 also improvises over cadenza chords: E9, E♭7(♭9), and A♭ Maj9.

So What—Miles Davis/Sweeney
Open solos. Changes written on all parts; written solo provided on separate sheet.

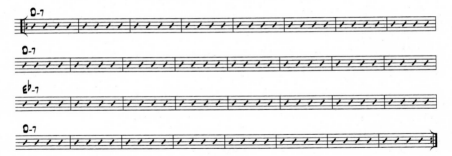

So What—Miles Davis/Taylor, M.
Open solos. (Changes written on Alto 1, Tenor 1, Baritone, Trumpet 2, Trombone 1, Guitar, Piano.
Written solos provided on a separate sheet.)

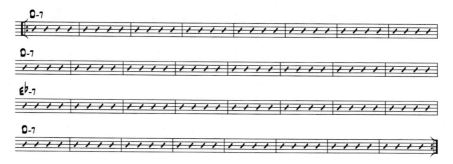

Song for My Father—Horace Silver/Taylor, M.
Written piano solo with changes.

Alto 1 solo first time, Tenor 1 or Trumpet 2 solo second time. Solos as written or ad lib.

Sonnymoon for Two—Sonny Rollins/Owen, S.
Alto 1 solo first time; Tenor 1 solo second time. All solos as written or ad lib.

Sophisticated Lady—"Duke" Ellington, Irving Mills, Mitchell Parish/Wolpe
Alto 1 solo fill (ballad tempo).

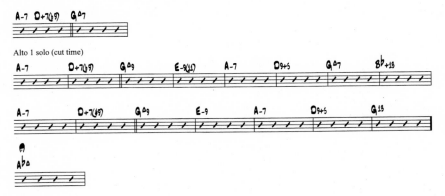

Soul Sister—Andy Sebesky/Clark, A.
Open solos.

Spain—Chick Corea/Jennings, P.
Open solos.

Splanky—Neal Hefti/Custer
Trombone 1 solo first time; Tenor 1 solo second time. Both solos as written or ad lib.

Written piano solo with changes.

Splanky—Neal Hefti/Phillipe
Piano solo as written or ad lib.

St. Louis Blues—William C. Handy/Davis, T.

Tenor 1 solo first time; Trombone 1 solo second time. Both solos as written or ad lib.

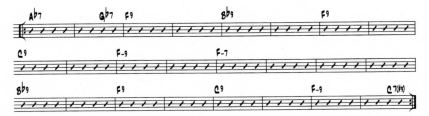

St. Louis Blues—William C. Handy/Norred

Optional solo for Alto 1 or Trumpet 2, as written or ad lib.

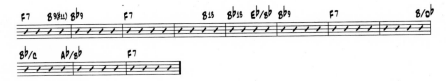

St. Thomas—Sonny Rollins/Sweeney

Trumpet 1 solo first time; Alto 1 solo second time. Both solos as written or ad lib.

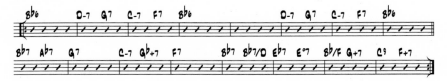

St. Thomas—Sonny Rollins/Taylor

Open solos. Written solos and chord changes provided on separate sheets.

Stolen Moments—Oliver Nelson/Blair

Solo for any saxophone as written or ad lib.

Stolen Moments—Oliver Nelson/Jennings, P.
Solo changes in Alto 1, Tenor 1, Trumpet 2, and Trombone 1. Alto 1 and Tenor 1 include both changes and a written solo.

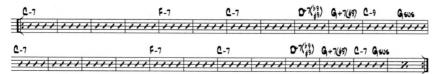

Stolen Moments—Oliver Nelson/Taylor, M.
Optional open solos. Written solos and chord changes provided on separate sheets.

Stompin' at the Savoy—Benny Goodman, Edgar Sampson, Chick Webb, Andy Razaf/Berry
Alto 1 solo first time; solo for any trumpet second time. Solos are as written or ad lib.

Stompin' at the Savoy—Benny Goodman, Edgar Sampson, Chick Webb, Andy Razaf/Sweeney
Trumpet 2 solo first time; Trombone 1 solo second time. Both solos as written or ad lib.

Straight, No Chaser—Thelonious Monk/Taylor
Open for solos. Changes in Tenor 1.

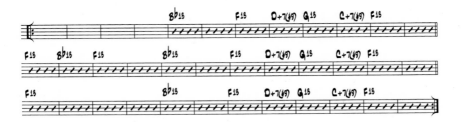

Sugar—Stanley Turrentine/Clarke, T.
Tenor 1 solo first time; Trumpet 2 solo second time. Both solos as written or ad lib.

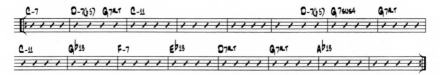

Sugar—Stanley Turrentine/Taylor, M.
Open solos. Written solos and chord changes provided on separate sheets.

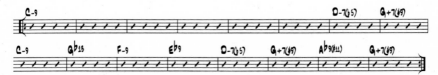

Summertime—George Gershwin, Dubose Heyward/Custer
Tenor 1 solo as written or ad lib.

Sweet Georgia Brown—Ben Bernie, Ken Casey, Maceo Pinkard/Lewis, M.
Written piano solo with changes.

Swingin' Shepherd Blues—Moe Kauffman, Rhoda Roberts, Kenny Jacobson/Phillipe
Piano solo first time; Trumpet 2 second time. Both solos as written or ad lib.

Alto 1 solo first time, Tenor 1 solo second time. Both solos as written or ad lib.

Swingin' Shepherd Blues—Moe Kauffman, Rhoda Roberts, Kenny Jacobson/Taylor
Trumpet 2 solo as written or ad lib.

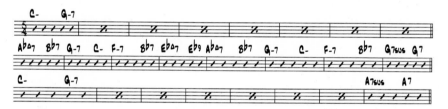

Take Five—Paul Desmond/Lewis, M.
Tenor 1 solo as written or ad lib.

Take Five—Paul Desmond/Wolpe
Alto 1 solo as written or ad lib. Parts and score incorrectly show a chord change occurring on beat five of each measure. The correct change, as shown in the bass line, occurs on beat four.

Take the A Train—Billy Strayhorn/Barduhn
Tenor 1 solo as written or ad lib.

Take the A Train—Billy Strayhorn/trans. Berger
Trumpet 2 solo as written or ad lib.

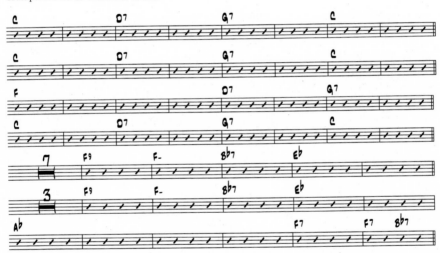

Take the A Train—Billy Strayhorn/Lowden
Tenor 1 solo as written or ad lib.

Take the A Train—Billy Strayhorn/Sweeney
Open solos as written or ad lib. Separate solo sheets provided.

Take the A Train—Billy Strayhorn/Taylor
Tenor 1 solo as written or ad lib.

Tenor Madness—Sonny Rollins/Berry
Trumpet 2 solo as written or ad lib.

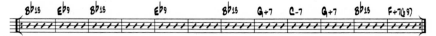

Things Ain't What They Used to Be—Mercer Ellington, Ted Persons/Lalama
Written piano solo with changes (8 mm.). Tenor 1 solo.

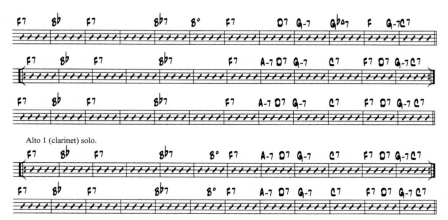

Things Ain't What They Used to Be—Mercer Ellington, Ted Persons/Mills
Piano solo.

Open solos.

This Can't Be Love—Richard Rogers, Lorenz Hart/Taylor
Trumpet 2 solo as written or ad lib.

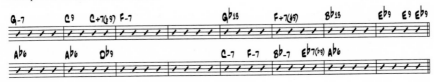

Triste—Antonio C. Jobim/Berg
Written piano solo with changes. Trumpet 2 or Tenor 1 solo.

Tuxedo Junction—Julian Dash, Buddy Feyne, Erskine Hawkins, William L. Johnson/Berry
Alto 1 solo as written or ad lib.

Until I Met You (Corner Pocket)—Freddie Green, Donald Wolf/Taylor, M.
Trumpet 2 solo as written or ad lib.

The Very Thought of You—Ray Noble/Stone
Trombone 1 solo as written or ad lib.

Walk, Don't Run—Shorty Rogers
Written piano solo with changes.

When I Fall in Love—Victor Young, Edward Heyman/Carubia
Alto 1 solo as written or ad lib.

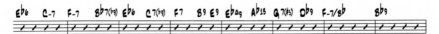

When You're Smiling—Mark Fisher, Larry Shay, Joe Goodwin/Kubis
Tenor 1 solo.

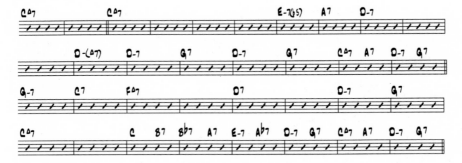

Woodchopper's Ball—Joe Bishop, Woody Herman/Blair
Alto 1 solo as written or ad lib.

Work Song—Nat Adderley, Oscar Brown Jr./Dana
Alto 1 solo first time; Trumpet 1 second time. Both solos as written or ad lib.

Yardbird Suite—Charlie Parker/Sweeney
Trumpet 2 solo as written or ad lib. Trumpet 2 part incorrectly indicates a G7 harmony from solo mm. 12*–15.

BIBLIOGRAPHY

Antrim, D. (1936). *Secrets of dance band success*. New York: Famous Stars.

Arnold, R. (1981). Curriculum corner: Curriculum K–12. *Jazz Educators Journal, 68*(1), 30.

Azzara, C. (1999). An aural approach to improvisation. *Music Educators Journal, 86*(3), 21–25.

Baker, D. (1988). *Jazz improvisation: A comprehensive method for all musicians*. Van Nuys, CA: Alfred.

Baker, D. (1989). *David Baker's jazz pedagogy: A comprehensive method of jazz education for teacher and student*. Van Nuys, CA: Alfred.

Baker, D. (1997). Pro session: Exercising options in improvisation. *Down Beat—Jazz, Blues & Beyond, 64*(3), 62–63.

Baker, D. (2003). IAJE president's message. *Jazz Education Journal, 36*(1), 4.

Berg, S. (1998). *Jazz improvisation: The goal note method*. Delevan, NY: Kendor Music.

Berg, S. (2002). Teaching resources . . . three excerpts: "Chop-monster." *Jazz Education Journal, 35*(1), 43.

Berliner, P. F. (1994). *Thinking in jazz: The infinite art of improvisation*. Chicago: University of Chicago.

Bitz, M. (1998). A description and investigation of strategies for teaching classroom music improvisation. *Dissertations Abstracts International, 59*(10), 3767A. (UMI No. 9909407)

Bruscia, K. E. (1987). *Improvisational models of music therapy.* Springfield, IL: Charles C. Thomas.

Campbell, W. (2000). Harmonic accuracy and the blues progression: Helping the maturing improviser. *Jazz Educators Journal, 32*(5), 53–54.

Caniato, M. (2005). Outstanding charts for jazz ensemble: Data from a recent survey. *Jazz Research Proceedings Yearbook, 25*, 59–64.

Carter, W. L. (1986). Jazz pedagogy: A history still in the making. *Jazz Educators Journal, 18*(4), 10–13, 49–50.

Choksy, L. (1999). *The Kodály method: Comprehensive music education from infant to adult* (3rd ed.). Englewood Cliffs, NJ: Prentice-Hall.

Collier, G., & Collier, J. (1996). Microrhythms in jazz: A review of papers. *Annual Review of Jazz Studies, 8*, 117–139.

Colnot, C. (1978). An open letter to the publishers of jazz ensemble music. *The Instrumentalist, 32*(6), 88.

Coy, D. A. (1989). A multisensory approach to teaching jazz improvisation to middle school band students. *Dissertations Abstracts International, 50*(11), 3508A. (UMI No. 9010106)

Crawford, R., & Magee, J. (1992). *Jazz standards on record, 1900–1942: A core repertory.* Chicago: Columbia College.

Day, W. (2000). Knowing as instancing: Jazz improvisation and moral perfectionism. *Journal of Aesthetics & Art Criticism, 58*(2), 99–112.

Dunscomb, J. R., & Hill, W. (2002). *Jazz pedagogy: The jazz educators handbook and resource guide.* Miami: Warner Brothers.

Dust, T. (2003). Good improvisation evolves from jazz forms, chord progressions. *The Instrumentalist, 57*(10), 17–19.

Fleming, L. A. (1994). *Getting started with jazz band.* Reston, VA: MENC.

Garcia, A. (1998). Grading jazz improvisation: On what basis? *Jazz Educators Journal, 30*(5), 61–64.

Garcia, A. (2002). More than the "changes": The practical side of a college jazz education. *Downbeat—Jazz, Blues & Beyond, 69*(10), 6–8, 10.

Hall, M. E. (1961). *Teacher's guide to the high school stage band.* Elkhart, IN: Selmer.

Hall, M. E. (1975). What's the score on jazz band charts? *Music Educators Journal, 62*(3), 75–80.

Horowitz, R. A. (1994). The development of a rating scale for jazz guitar improvisation performance. *Dissertations Abstracts International, 55*(11), 3443A. (UMI No.9511046)

Hynes, T. (2000). Melody and melodicism in the teaching of jazz improvisation. *Jazz Educators Journal, 32*(6), 46–49.

IAJE-MTNA Alliance Committee (2001). *IAJE-MTNA jazz studies guide.* Cincinnati, OH: Music Teachers National Association.

Janowiak, J. (2000). Jazz education guide: What is a jazz education today? *Down Beat—Jazz, Blues & Beyond, 67*(10), S6–S8, S10–S11.

Jarvis, J. (2000). Tips on publishing jazz charts. *The Instrumentalist, 54*(10), 58, 60.

Johnson-Laird, P. N. (2002). How jazz musicians improvise. *Music Perception, 19*(3), 415–442.

Kanellopoulos, P. A. (1999). Children's conception and practice of musical improvisation. *Psychology of Music, 27*(2), 175–191.

Kuzmich, J. (2004). Kudos to the Associated Board of the Royal Schools of Music: An innovative international jazz curriculum. *Jazz Education Journal, 36*(6), 70–72.

Kuzmich, J., & Bash, L. (1984). *Complete guide to instrumental jazz instruction.* West Nyack, NY: Parker.

Kynaston, T. P., & Ricci, R. J. (1978). *Jazz improvisation.* Englewood Cliffs, NJ: Prentice-Hall.

LaPorta, J. (1965). *Developing the school jazz ensemble.* Boston: Berklee Press.

Laughlin, J. E. (2001). The use of notated and aural exercises as pedagogical procedures intended to develop harmonic accuracy among beginning jazz improvisers. *Dissertations Abstracts International, 63*(02), 534A. (UMI No. 3042832)

Levine, M. (1995). *The jazz theory book.* Petaluma, CA: Sher Music.

Luty, B. (1982). Jazz education's struggle for acceptance. *Music Educators Journal, 69*(3), 38–39, 53.

Luty, B. (1982). Jazz ensembles' era of accelerated growth. *Music Educators Journal, 69*(4), 49–50, 64.

Mark, M. L. (1975). In and out of the mainstream. *Music Educators Journal, 62*(3), 62–67.

Mark, M. L. (1987). The acceptance of jazz in the music education curriculum: A model for interpreting a historical process. *Bulletin for Research in Music Education, 2*(3), 15–21.

Mark, M. L., & Gary, C. (1999). *A history of American music education.* Reston, VA: MENC.

MENC & International Association of Jazz Educators (1996). *Teaching jazz: A course of study.* Reston, VA: MENC.

National Arts Education Association. (1994). *Standards for arts education: What every young American should know and be able to do in the arts.* Reston, VA: Author.

Parker, C. (1978). *Charlie Parker omnibook* (J. Aebersold & K. Slone, Eds.). Hollywood, CA: Atlantic Music.

Pavlicevic, M. (2000). Improvisation in music therapy: Human communication in sound. *Journal of Music Therapy, 37*(4), 269–285.

Perry, M. R. (2003). Relating improvisational music therapy with severely and multiply disabled children to communication development. *Journal of Music Therapy, 40*(3), 227–246.

Radocy, R. E., & Boyle, J. D. (2003). *Psychological foundations of musical behavior.* Springfield, IL: Charles C. Thomas.

Sawyer, R. K. (1999). Improvised conversations: Music, collaboration, and development. *Psychology of Music, 27*(2), 192–205.

Schleuter, S. L. (1997). *A sound approach to teaching instrumentalists: An application of content and learning sequences.* New York: Schirmer.

Smeijsters, H., & van den Hurk, J. (1999). Music therapy helping to work through grief and finding a personal identity. *Journal of Music Therapy, 36*(3), 222–252.

Thelonious Monk Institute of Jazz. (n.d.). *History of jazz education, a brief outline.* Retrieved December 14, 2004, from http://www.jazzinamerica.org/1_jazzed.asp.

Thelonious Monk Institute of Jazz launches Jazz in America: The National Jazz Curriculum. *Jazz Educators Journal, 32*(5), March 2000, p. 24.

Tirro, F. (1974). Constructive elements in jazz improvisation. *Journal of the American Musicological Society, 27*(2), 285–305.

Welch, G. F. (1999). Education and musical improvisation: In response to Keith Sawyer. *Psychology of Music, 27*(2), 211–214.

Williams, M., & Richards, D. (1988). Jazz classics: The missing essential in jazz education. *Bulletin of the Council for Research in Music Education, 96*, 1–6.

Wiskirchen, G. C. (1961). *Developmental techniques for the school dance band.* Boston: Berklee Press.

Wiskirchen, G. C. (1975). If we're going to teach jazz, we must teach improvisation. *Music Educators Journal, 62*(3), 68–74.

Zaworski, D. (2000). Jazz on campus: Monk Institute effort extends jazz ed to all U.S. public schools. *Down Beat—Jazz, Blues & Beyond, 67*(3), 78.

Zwick, R. A. (1987). Jazz improvisation: A recommended sequential format of instruction. *Dissertations Abstracts International, 48*(03), 592A. (UMI No. 8713994)

ABOUT THE AUTHOR

Zachary Poulter is band director at Syracuse Junior High School in Syracuse, Utah, where he directs beginning bands, two concert bands, percussion ensemble, and jazz ensemble. His interest in building students' independent musicianship and interdependent performance skills has led to the development of additional small ensembles, including jazz combos, as well as innovative class projects in composition and film scoring. He is active as a guest performer in both classical and jazz styles, a clinician (especially in the areas of classroom management and jazz pedagogy), and an adjudicator.

Poulter is a graduate of Ricks College (now known as Brigham Young University–Idaho, AS), Brigham Young University (BM), and the University of Utah (MM).